Classics Teaching in Europe

Classics Teaching in Europe

Edited by

John Bulwer

Duckworth

First published in 2006 by
Gerald Duckworth & Co. Ltd.
90-93 Cowcross Street, London EC1M 6BF
Tel: 020 7490 7300
Fax: 020 7490 0080
inquiries@duckworth-publishers.co.uk
www.ducknet.co.uk

A catalogue record for this book is available
from the British Library

ISBN 0 7156 3560 3
EAN 9780715635605

Typeset by e-type, Liverpool
Printed and bound in Great Britain by
MPG Books Limited, Bodmin

Contents

Preface

John Bulwer

This book is intended for all practising Classics teachers in all European countries so that we may all know a little more about each others' practices and traditions, and so that we may reflect on our own and even borrow other people's ideas if we think they could be useful.

It is also intended for an audience of students training for the teaching of Classics in all these European countries, and for their teachers and for practising Classicists in universities. Perhaps it may additionally be of use to politicians and administrators taking decisions about Classics in their countries' curriculum. They may see that the convictions they hold so firmly are not necessarily all shared by others in different countries. Views on the usefulness, for example, of learning ancient languages for the acquisition of modern ones vary sharply from one state to another.

The contributors wish to provide a snapshot of the situation for Classical Studies in a wide variety of European countries halfway through the first decade of the twenty-first century. It is hoped that the book will be also a contribution to the already long history of Classical Studies in Europe.

All chapters have been written in English. This seems to be a necessity if all readers in each contributing country are to be able to read the contributions of the others. English is in a way the new Latin. We could perhaps have submitted our contributions in Latin, but even specialists may find it easier to cope with English. Some have been professionally translated, some have been written directly in English by non-native speakers and some I have translated. I have corrected and edited all contributions, but some infelicities may still remain for which I take responsibility. My thanks and admiration is due to all the contributing teachers who have bravely used their second or third language.

Not every country has been included. I should like to have included more but for various reasons plans fell through and contributions did not become available from some.

I should like to thank all those who have contributed to this project, particularly Deborah Blake and James Morwood for setting off the idea and for giving invaluable support. Thanks also to all the contributors for their patience and forbearance, and to others who have helped with the project, read over some of the material and given their suggestions:

Classics Teaching in Europe

Annie Van Praet, Senno Verduijn, Paul Ieven, Veerle De Troyer, Julian Morgan, Mathieu de Bakker, Stefano Moia, Chloe Bulwer and Regina Loidolt.

Notes on Contributors

Editor and United Kingdom
John Bulwer teaches Classics, Philosophy and English at the European School, Uccle, Brussels, Belgium. He has worked with colleagues and taught pupils from almost all countries of the EU. He has researched and published articles on language learning in a multilingual environment and on the reception of Classics in modern literature. He was JACT (Joint Association of Classical Teachers) representative of Euroclassica, and then treasurer and secretary (1995-2003). He has given workshops and papers at many international conferences.

Austria
Alfred Reitermayer teaches Latin at a high school in the eastern part of Styria, Austria. He is active in the Austrian Classical teachers' association: *Sodalitas* (*Bundesarbeitsgemeinschaft klassischer Philologen in Öster-reich*) and is its representative on the Executive Committee of Euroclassica. He is active in negotiations with politicians in Austria about the position of Latin in the national curriculum, and in the creation of a European Curriculum for Classics.

Belgium
Fabienne Paternotte, Colette Goedert, Catherine Brux and Noëlle Hanegreefs are teachers from different types of school in French-speaking Belgium. Between them they have a wide experience of teaching Latin and Greek at all levels in secondary schools. They are members of the FPGL (*Fédération des Professeurs de Grec et de Latin*).

Liesbet Waumans studied Classical Philology at the RUG (University of Ghent). She taught Latin and Greek for 20 years. From 2000 she has been working for the Flemish Department of Education as an inspector in the Flemish Inspectorate.

Joeri Facq also graduated at the RUG. He teaches Latin and Greek at the Koninlijk Atheneum in Sint-Niklaas, and is a member of the board of VLOT (*Vereniging Leraren Oude Talen*, Association of Teachers of Classical Languages), which has members in all kinds of Flemish school systems (the official and free educational schools).

Croatia

Zlatko Šešelj studied Classical Philology at the Faculty of Philosophy, University of Zagreb. Since his graduation in 1975 he has taught Latin and Greek in elementary schools and high schools. In 1996 he founded a private Classical High School, which he still runs today and where he also teaches Latin and Greek. He started a journal called *Latina et Graeca*, and has been its editor-in-chief since the third issue (in 1974). Since 1979 he has been an editor-in-chief of Biblioteka L&G, which has so far published around a hundred volumes (bilingual editions, scientific and specialised books in the field of Classical Studies). He has written bibliographical works, lexicon contributions, translations and other articles. He is a co-author of a series of Latin textbooks. He has also published stories from Greek mythology for young children. He is engaged in efforts to improve the position of Latin and Greek in the Croatian educational system, and is also involved in a number of international educational projects.

Czech Republic

Barbara Pokorná is a senior lecturer at the Department of Classical Philology at the Palacky University in Olomouc. She studied Latin and Czech Language at the Philosophical Faculty of Masaryk University in Brno (1981-6), and in 1988 started to teach Czech language for foreign students, and Latin medical terminology for students of medicine. Since 1992 she has been teaching Latin syntax and history of ancient art at the Department of Classical Philology. Since 1999 she has been working for the international organisation Euroclassica as a member of its Executive Committee and representative of ALFA (*Antiquis Linguis Fovendis Associatio*).

Denmark

Elisabeth Nedergaard studied Latin and Greek at the University of Odense, 1975-83. She teaches Classics at upper secondary school level, at Noerresundby Gymnasium. Apart from teaching, Elisabeth Nedergaard has been actively involved in the Classical Association in Denmark and has played an active role regarding the integration of ICT in Classics in Denmark as a partner in the international CIRCE project, a Comenius 2.1 project about ICT in Classics at a European level.

France

Odile Denis-Laroque is a teacher of Classics (*professeur de lettres classiques*) with *agrégation* in Classical literature. She has taught Latin, Greek and French in different schools in Le Mans and has also taught preparatory classes in French for entry to university, and Greek at the University of Maine. She taught at the European School in Uccle, Brussels, and is now teaching at the Lycée Franco-Allemand de Buc in Versailles.

Germany

Hans-Joachim Glücklich is director of the Department of Classics in the Rhineland-Palatinate Seminary for Student Teachers, Mainz; since 1982 he has been Professor of Didactics of Latin and Greek at the University of Heidelberg (Germany); member of the executive committee of DAV (*Deutscher Altphilologen Verband*); and from 1999 to 2003 president of Euroclassica. He has published many books on teaching practice and Latin texts for students (with commentary for teachers) of Caesar, Catullus, Plautus, Virgil, Nepos, Terence, Cicero, Ovid, Sallust and Pliny the Younger.

Italy

Annarella Perra has taught Ancient Greek and Latin in a *Liceo Classico* from 1988 and has been involved in the ICT world for a long time, with a special interest in e-learning and in ICT and Classics (as a tutor and teacher trainer). From 2001 she has been a lecturer in ICT and Classics at SSIS, the pre-service teaching department of the University of Cagliari, and represents the Italian partner (CIRD-SSIS, University of Cagliari) in the CIRCE Project.

Latvia

Vita Paparinska is a professor in the Department of Classical Philology, University of Latvia. She has been teaching Classics since 1977. As director of the Bachelor Programme in Classical Philology (since 1995) she is responsible for the contents and practical implementation of the programme, as well as for teaching Latin and Greek language and literature to the undergraduate and graduate students of the programme. Her main research areas are Greek and Roman prose and epic poetry and poetry of the Hellenistic age. She has published articles on Greek and Hellenistic poetry and Roman historical prose in collections of readings on Classical languages and literature (published by the Department of Classical Philology, University of Latvia).

Gita Berzina is a lecturer in the Department of Classical Philology, University of Latvia. She has been teaching Classics since 1996. She is responsible for the general primary Latin and Greek course curriculum and for teaching Latin and Greek languages and literature to the undergraduate and graduate students of the Classical Philology programme. Her main research areas are Latin poetry of the Augustan Age, Greek and Latin epic poetry and Greek prose. She has published articles on Greek prose in collections of readings on Classical languages and literature (published by the Department of Classical Philology, University of Latvia).

The Netherlands

Egge Tijsseling studied at Utrecht and has taught Latin and Greek at a number of *Gymnasia* in the Netherlands. He is the Euroclassica representative for the VCN (*Vereniging Classici Nederland*), the Dutch association of Classical teachers, and has been responsible for the national examinations in Greek.

Portugal

Francisco de Oliveira is a professor at the Institute for Classical Studies, University of Coimbra, Portugal. He is a member of the Centre for Classical and Humanistic Studies of the University of Coimbra and of the *Centre d'Études et de Représentations du Théâtre Antique* (*CERTA*) of the *Université de Bretagne Occidentale*, France. He is a former dean of the Faculty of Letters (1996-2002), current president of Euroclassica, president of the Portuguese Association for Classical Studies, and director of the Institute for Classical Studies. He is also a director of teacher training programmes, including in-service training. He has spoken at conferences in many countries and has many publications in Portuguese, French, Spanish, English and German.

Aires Pereira do Couto is a professor at the Portuguese Catholic University. He is director of the Faculty of Arts, director of teacher training programmes and a member of the board of the Portuguese Association for Classical Studies. His research subjects are Latin literature (Plautus, Terence and Horace) and Neo-Latin literature in Portugal.

Romania

Gabriela Cretia teaches in the Classical Philology Department, University of Bucharest. Her doctoral thesis, '*Dignus et ses dérivés. Étude de lexicologie diachronique latine*', was published in French (Bucharest University Press, 2003). She has taught historical Latin grammar and history of language, as well as Latin lexicology, Vulgar Latin, and stylistics. She has maintained contact with teaching in high schools, as president of the National Commission of the Ministry of Education (1992-8) and of numerous Ministerial Commissions for national contests or for First Degree examinations of Latin teachers. She is the author of Latin manuals used in Romanian high schools. She has participated in numerous international congresses and has published many books and articles in the field of Classics. She is the Romanian representative in Euroclassica, having been a member of its Executive Committee between 1990 and 1998, and is currently vice-president of the Romanian Society of Classical Studies (*Societatea de Studii Clasice din Romania*).

Cristian Emilian Ghita studied at the Faculty of Foreign Languages and Literature, Classical Philology Department, at the University of Bucharest. He has been awarded the Leventis Foundation Scholarship for a PhD course at the University of Exeter. He has taught both Latin and World Literature in Bucharest. His articles have been published in *Nova*

Studia Classica, a collection of studies by young Romanian Classicists, and in *Convorbiri Literare*.

Spain

José Luis Navarro teaches Greek at the Carlos III National Lyceum in Madrid. He is an associate professor at the University of Madrid in Classics education. He is also a tutor for the Open University of Spain in Greek Language and Literature and for the Open University of Greece in Spanish Language and Civilisation. He has published Latin and Greek texts for the Spanish Baccalaureate, and translations of Greek tragedy and comedy and of other prose and poetry. He has directed many productions of Greek drama, and has been on the committees of the SEEC (*Sociedad Española de Estudios Clásicos*) and Euroclassica.

Sweden

Eva Schough Tarandi teaches Latin with general knowledge of language and German at Kungsholmens Gymnasium in Stockholm. She studied at Stockholm University, and was then a member of the Stockholm University Classical Department. She has been a member of the *Svenska Klassikerförbundet* for many years and has been a member of the Euroclassica Executive Committee since 1999, as vice-president since 2003. She organises Academia Latina, the Euroclassica summer school in Rome.

Introduction

John Bulwer

Teaching has for many years been organised by nation states. Since the introduction of compulsory education for all took place in the era of strong nations in the nineteenth and twentieth centuries, it has been regarded as natural for these states to decide who should be educated, to what level, to which age, and in which subjects. Teaching is professionalised and regulated by qualification. Many professionals remain rooted in their own traditions, in their own countries, even in their own regions or cities. Professionals may fairly ask themselves how much they know about what goes on in other schools in other countries, even in their own subjects. We may assume that mathematics, for example, cannot change much from country to country as the knowledge base is the same. Yet we may find that the approach to mathematics can vary significantly in different states owing to a number of cultural and ideological factors. If we took a curriculum area such as mother tongue or first language learning we might expect to find highly significant differences, even though the subject is ostensibly the same one. What goes on in a class labelled French on a timetable in a school in Paris will contrast sharply with what goes on in a class labelled English in a school in Edinburgh. Yet marks will be given and qualifications accorded which will have currency in an international job market. It is worth considering what exactly we mean by these final pedagogical judgements.

This volume attempts to put together a number of accounts of the world of Classics teaching in different European countries. The contributors speak in their own words about what they understand of their own system and traditions. Classics is no longer the basis of all education that it once was. The foundations and methods of learning that it set out in the early years of mass education have now been superseded by new subject areas which often have their origin in one or other part of Classics, but which now have become real subjects in their own rights. As a result the father figure has been eclipsed and has seen his children grow up and become independent. There has been a natural reaction for these upstart children to deny the achievements and status of the father figure in order to justify their own arrival at adulthood, and so we must wait for the cycle to roll round a little further for the study of the ancient world in all its aspects to establish its new position in the curriculum. However, its position in the

1

European education system needs to be charted at this stage in its long development in order for a full view of its situation to emerge. It seems that similar pressures are being exerted on the subject in many countries, but that they develop at different rates. In addition the variety of approaches, particularly towards language learning, emerges from these reports, showing the different attitudes adopted in each state. The status of the mother tongue of the country is particularly significant here.

Some countries see Classics as an essentially European subject: one that shows how their own country is linked to all the others in the European Union and beyond, and which ties all those in the wider European family together. Others see Classics as a subject which transmits high culture and which inculcates civilised values in its citizens. Some following this same path extend this to a view of Classics as an elitist and undemocratic subject which divides its citizens. (This view used to be particularly prevalent in the UK, although many realise now that the decline has gone so far that this perception can no longer be maintained, and that a minority taste for the study of ancient civilisations might have something to be said for it after all.) Some countries, often in the north of Europe, without a long and developed tradition of Classical Studies, regard the subject as a slightly eccentric pursuit, rather like Egyptology, and thus Classicists there have no inherited baggage to carry concerning class structures and elitism. Others have an additional complication if they happen to be predominantly Catholic countries. Here the role of Latin in the Catholic Church plays a sometimes unwanted role. Latin may here be seen as part of the culture of Catholicism with all its concomitant cultural baggage. Many of the following chapters reveal the role of politics in the place of Classics in the national curriculum. Of course political considerations are fundamental to all educational decisions, but it is worth noting how different countries attach political significance to Classics. In some it can be the left which is generally opposed to Classical Studies, in others the reverse. In general people see in Classics a reflection of what else they see in their own particular society. Usually what is actually going on in Classics lessons in all European countries is far from what the country mythologises as Classics. The Classics teacher undergoing an existential breakdown in Cees Nooteboom's *Het volgende Verhaal* (The Following Story) is very different from Mr Chips in James Hilton's *Goodbye Mr Chips*. Yet this last gives many English people their stereotype for the Latin teacher (Leary 2004).

Language learning

Some, we shall see, maintain a tradition of Classics, often of Latin, seeing it as an essential part of language learning, both for the mother tongue and for the acquisition of foreign languages. This may occur in countries where the mother tongue is not widely spoken outside that country, like the Netherlands; but also in countries where the language is based on Latin and where a high premium is placed on a profound knowledge of the grammar and structure of the mother tongue, like France. This can also be the case in Germany and Austria, where the language is not Latin-based, but where a high premium is placed on foreign language learning and on high culture. Other countries can still place a strong emphasis on the acquisition of Latin and Greek as useful tools for other subjects, particularly medicine and science, as well as modern foreign languages and history. This transfer of skills from one subject to another, particularly the argument for Latin and/or Greek as an aid for learning modern languages, is currently out of favour in English-speaking countries. However, as will be seen, it is taken seriously elsewhere. In Sweden the official government programme for Latin specifically mentions this aspect of the subject: modern languages and scientific terminology. Latin and English are seen as complementary in one area of Germany (the *Biberacher Modell*). It must be admitted that English-speaking countries are not renowned at present for their skills in learning and speaking languages other than English. The decline of Latin and Greek learning in school has not been accompanied by a compensatory rise in foreign language learning.

Terminology

There is a problem of terminology in this subject area which must be addressed. Classics is a term which has overtones of approval, even of elitism. Derived from a Latin word (rather than Greek which supplies most other subject names), its name implies first-class or top-rank (Wiseman 2002, preface). Other countries supply a bewildering variety of other terms: *lettres classiques, Altphilologie, Altertumswissenschaft, klassieke talen, KCV*, and so on. Some talk only of Latin and Greek, others of Classical Studies or Classical Civilisation. The English expression used in the different contributions may give some clue as to the attitude of the particular country. One country may use *Latin and Greek* as opposed to *Classics*, for example. This perhaps reveals a closer concentration on linguistic learning than on the study of the whole of the ancient world. However, some contributors have composed their pieces directly in English, while others have written in their first language and then used a professional translator. Others have been written in close collaboration with a native speaker of English. This may have led to some nuances being lost in translation. The different chapters may help us decide if we are in fact all talking about the same thing, or whether the national traditions put so much of a different emphasis on the subject that it in fact turns into something else. The tradition in certain countries (France and Italy, for example) of entrusting some of the teaching of the mother tongue to teachers who are also trained in teaching the ancient languages has a considerable effect on the way that Classics is regarded within the education system.

A new term seems to be beginning to emerge in English: Ancient Civilisations. Perhaps we may begin to talk about Ancient Civilisations and Languages as a subject area, but we shall never entirely get rid of 'Classics' with all its baggage, and positive and negative connotations. One phrase that does seem to have finally fallen out of use is that of a 'classical education'. This has overtones of the nineteenth-century English public school, where Classics in some form or other made up the lion's share of the timetable. One of the founders of the English *Classical Association* (J.P. Postgate) foresaw this back in 1902 (Stray 2003). It should be borne in mind here that this type of education refers to a way in which general education for young boys (mainly) was delivered by means of learning ancient languages. Thus grammar, reading, writing and comprehension, and even creative expression (through verse composition) were taught by masters through Latin (or Greek). Rather than regard a character such as Mr Chips (Leary 2004) as a Classical specialist, we should recognise that his job was to instruct junior boys as a general master in the basics of language and expression; not to engage in the sort of critical interpretation of ambiguities in Ovid or Greek Tragedy that we may be more used to today (with older students). It would be quite mistaken to compare what happens in Classics classrooms today with a 'classical education' of the past. Regret at the very real decline in numbers taking Latin should be tempered by the fact that the numbers taking Classical subjects today have opted in to them and generally are there in the class because they want to be there, rather than because Latin was the way in which they learned the basics of everything. No one would support a return to this method of learning. The number of real students of Classical subjects – specialists who have an enthusiasm for their chosen area of study – may not have changed as drastically as we think. In some countries, as can be seen in the contribution from France, the widening of access to Classical languages to pupils of all abilities may even have raised the numbers who begin Latin, even though many of them do not continue to follow it until the end of their schooling.

A national curriculum

In many countries the education programme for state schools is a matter of centralised governmental control. To those who are used to considerable freedom, and where individual schools are allowed to decide on their curriculum, this may come as a surprise. Equally, those for whom the curriculum is dictated by an all-powerful ministry of education may be astonished that the age for starting Latin may be varied by even as much as a year in individual schools. The attitude of the particular country towards this question will emerge from the way the piece is phrased, as will the way that a country's recent history plays an important part even in something as politically insignificant as the teaching of Classics. Spain, for example, traces changes in the teaching of Latin to the death of Franco. Romania, on the other hand, sees the communist post-war dominance as a crucial element in the question of the survival of Latin and Greek. Some contributions will show that teachers in a particular country will regard it as entirely natural that its government should decide how many hours per week are given to a particular subject. Others will show that they think it natural that each school should decide such things.

Public attitudes

Classics has to live with its reputation among the general public. This attitude is often several steps behind the reality of what actually happens in the classroom, but people's attitudes are often formed by their own schooling and they tend to keep these preconceptions through their adult life. This kind of attitude emerges in the contributions. Often Classics has the reputation of being an elitist subject, giving a mark of a high level of educational achievement. It may even be a mark of class distinction, showing that a pupil attended a particular sort of school, possibly one reserved for the middle classes. This reputation often goes with a reported decline in the number of those studying Latin. This would appear to be a contradiction, the belief seeming to be that if the mark of distinction were removed the distinctions would disappear. This is of course a false hope as the middle classes always find new ways to distinguish themselves from the majority of the population.

There is an alternative solution: to extend the distinguishing feature to a wider majority and to make the high level of education available to all. This is the solution which most Classics teachers would support, as the thing that unites them is a desire to have more students in their classes. An argument often cited against the wider dissemination of Classics among the general school population is the alleged difficulty of the subject, particularly the languages. Some contributions deal with this question in the light of the changes in education in the 1960s and 1970s, when the former selective systems of education were abandoned in favour of comprehensive schemes where pupils of all abilities are taught together. Several contributions report less than enthusiastic support for Classics from their governments. However, when political action is launched and government decisions challenged there is often considerable public support for Classics reported in the media and in public debate. Recent reforms in France have caused a debate in the press with articles and petitions circulated, the details of which are at www.cnarela.asso.fr. Belgium has also recently mobilised opinion in the face of a reform to the educational system (www.fpgl.be) (Centre Jean Gol 2005). Another public attitude in certain countries is the connection often seen between Latin and the Catholic Church. This is not a problem which occurs in Protestant countries. Again, given the humanistic and secular approach of many teachers of Classics across Europe, this is a perception which is far behind the reality of what happens in the classroom.

Pronunciation

This has been a controversial topic for centuries and it was said that at certain periods one scholar could not understand the pronunciation of Latin of another from a different country. However, in these chapters there now seems to be a remarkable agreement on the *pronuntiatio restituta*. Individual teachers, it must be admitted, can also use idiosyncratic pronunciations which will only be detected when the pupil moves out of that particular classroom. Parents from different nationalities can also have quite fixed ideas about this and feel that the way they learnt is the only correct way. Italy is one country where this is still a highly pertinent question. The close relation between Latin and modern Italian and the continued use of it by the Vatican mean that an Italianate pronunciation is often current in the classroom. However, the concept of the *pronuntiatio restituta* is well known and accepted by many professional Classicists who use it in their classrooms (Mandruzzato 1989, Allen 1978). A recent international conference in Italy on 'Living Latin' or the use of the direct method showed that the reformed pronunciation is current in many countries and so speakers were intelligible to each other (Orr 1998). Some writers show that awareness of classroom practice and innovation is current in Italy (Miraglia 1996, Rossi 1996, Bettini 1995) although their pioneering tone implies that they are addressing an audience to whom a lot of what they have to say is unfamiliar. Attempts at using Latin as a modern spoken language for direct communication (a capacity which some Classicists have) tend to attract some slightly mocking publicity, and can be the preserve of those with slightly dubious political views. Most professional Classicists tend to avoid this, although the direct method continues to have its champions. Nevertheless, the sound of Latin is important in the classroom and however much an ideal pronunciation is aimed for, native accents still have an effect on the way each individual pronounces Latin. Only Sweden seems to mention an awareness of different pronunciations at different historical periods as a stated educational aim in the official syllabus (Schough Tarandi, this volume). In the end it is probably not possible ever to reach a fully authentic original manner of pronunciation. Allen (1978) has some illuminating comments on the pronunciation of Latin in different European countries (in Appendix B of *Vox Latina* – second edition). Perhaps we can only aim at what would be a suitable or authentic accent for the historical context of the text under consideration. However, it is still not easy to decide, for example, what would be a suitable pronunciation for the choir to use in a performance of Carl Orff's

Catulli Carmina: authentic Catullan of the first century BCE or the kind of sounds used in a German *Gymnasium* of the 1930s?

In many European countries the generally recognised, reformed and authentic pronunciation of Greek is known as the pronunciation of Erasmus, its origin being traced back to the Renaissance scholar of Rotterdam in his dialogue: *De recta Latini Graecique sermonis pronuntiatione* of 1528. This pronunciation is recognised in nearly all countries as the authentic way to pronounce Ancient Greek. However, in Greece itself some teachers will use the Modern Greek pronunciation for Ancient Greek, on grounds of familiarity and ease of learning for the students. Indeed this method has been recommended by others as a method of learning both ancient and modern forms of the language at once. In the end even most Greek teachers of Ancient Greek will agree that the sounds of Modern Greek do not reproduce the Athenian Attic of the fifth century and that a revised pronunciation is probably more authentic. This is a question that can rouse considerable passion.

Latin, Greek and Classical Civilisation

There is variation among the countries as to what actually the subject consists of. In some countries the emphasis is on the language learning and the non-linguistic content is seen as an add-on. In others the learning about the society in which the ancient languages were spoken is just as important and is considered as going hand in hand with the language learning. A concentration on Latin only can lead to a view which sees the language in all its forms from Roman times through medieval and on up to modern times as the subject under consideration. This is the line taken by Françoise Waquet in *Latin or the Empire of a Sign* (Waquet 1998/2001), where the author concentrates on the teaching and learning of Latin from the sixteenth to the twentieth centuries, and neglects Classical Studies entirely. This leads her to some strange conclusions, such as the premature claim that Latin need be learnt only to read Neo-Latin texts as the Classical ones have been translated already. This extraordinary conclusion could be reached only by someone who divorces the language from the culture that produced it. The majority of the pieces from the contributors show that the study of Latin in schools is centred on the study of the language and culture of ancient Mediterranean civilisation, and is not an abstract language theory class. Latin in any later form (medieval, Renaissance or other) is for the specialists of the particular area concerned (for example, History of Science, Theology or Philosophy). Greek is a different case (ignored by Waquet in spite of its traditional place alongside Latin) and classes may well be concentrated more on language learning. Greek is nearly always begun after Latin and there may be greater exposure to Greek culture in Classical Civilisation courses or elsewhere. Greek Tragedy (in translation), for instance, is included in many Theatre Studies courses. Students who decide they need Greek language as well may come to it knowing what they are letting themselves in for. Intensive language demands can then be made and responded to. Overall, however, there have been shifts of attitude in many countries which lead to language and civilisation elements being treated alongside each other at all times.

Elitism and utilitarianism

This is a problem which teachers in many countries face. Learning the ancient languages is difficult and Classical Civilisation is seen as representative of high culture. It is, therefore, seen as a subject fit only for pupils of the highest ability. The schools which take these pupils are seen as middle class and exclusive. The twentieth century has been a time of extension of education provision to all classes and abilities. Among all the changes which have taken place in education in European countries in recent times, Classical subjects have been seen as representing the old systems and have been put under pressure and squeezed out of the timetable. Abolishing Latin is often shorthand for modernising the education system. It is a curious argument. It seems to say that if Classical subjects are removed from the timetable then education generally will become more inclusive and all class distinctions will be removed. In fact when this line of thinking is put under public scrutiny it usually collapses, and government ministers profess public commitment to the study of Classical subjects (they can hardly be seen to be in favour of ignorance and low standards). However, it does not mean that they become enthusiastic supporters and actually do anything to help. Their bland professions soon vanish into thin air.

In addition the contributions make it clear how far teachers all over Europe have gone to make Classical subjects forward-looking, inclusive and attractive. Perhaps they have modernised themselves rather more than teachers of other subjects which have a secure place on the timetable and thus have no need to compete for pupils. In certain countries where Latin and Classics have a more secure timetable place and where it may even be an obligatory subject in some sections, the skills of recruitment and retention that are highlighted by Eva Schough Tarandi (this volume) may play a smaller part. The general trend, however, shown in nearly all contributions in this book is for some retrenchment in the teaching of Classics in the face of competition from other subjects. The move towards Classics becoming an optional subject may mean that all Classics teachers should pay close attention to marketing programmes and devices to make the subject attractive to young people so that they will wish to opt in to it for its own sake. Those countries where this has been a necessity for a number of years, as is the case in the USA and the UK, can perhaps make suggestions and provide examples to those where it may soon be needed (LaFleur 1998, Morwood 2003).

Introduction

Several countries hint that Latin is continued in some schools to give them an appearance of high standards of learning and discipline which is attractive to some parents. While most teachers of Classics would deplore this kind of snobbery, as teachers of a subject under considerable pressure they would probably welcome some support and not worry too much about which quarter it comes from. It is even possible that a country may see nothing wrong with an elitist education. Just such a phenomenon is recently reported from the Netherlands, where the *Gymnasium* with its pre-university entrance stream has compulsory Latin and Greek. This system is popular with parents who like the traditional Dutch academic education it offers (Crump, in Lister, forthcoming). It may also be added that even though this may be an elitist education, it is offered to all in state-funded schools. The problems of class distinction in private schools where the most demanding and elitist education is only available to those who pay for it does not arise in those countries where education is a state institution.

In most other cases justification for the inclusion of a subject on the timetable is almost always utilitarian. Parents want to be confident that what their children learn at school will be useful for them in the future. This can lead them to some curious conclusions, as they appear to believe that a lot of material studied at a fairly advanced stage of school will be actually used by the pupils in their future careers. The rapid pace of change in many areas means that almost all of this material will be out of date by the time these pupils enter the world of work. However, abstract or theoretical material which does not change is unlikely to be actually used by anyone but the most advanced specialist. Most advanced mathematics and science is as abstract and theoretical as a Latin text, perhaps more so. Much more important in this kind of area of education are the advanced thinking skills, the organisation and interpretation of difficult material and the production of reasoned and balanced conclusions from evidence. As we all know, Classics can play as a good a part in this kind of education as any other subject. Employers generally want to recruit good graduates in any subjects who have demonstrated that they can think and reason well and can deal with demanding tasks in a satisfactory manner. The actual subject studied at advanced level is usually of little relevance. Parents and students are still over-intent on the immediate use of a subject to a possible future career, and need convincing that education at the higher level is more than simply training. Many students go to study Classics at university for its own sake, not to become professional Classicists. They go on to many different professions (see for the UK *Degree Course Guide to Classics*, CRAC 2003).

Utilitarianism also has its own drawbacks. Its concentration on the greatest good for the greatest number poses problems for minorities and those who have a strong commitment to a particular subject but who cannot be accommodated alongside the greater numbers who opt for the more popular subjects. If a student genuinely does not want to study what everyone else does but opts for something else, his or her wishes are ignored under a utilitarian system which emphasises conformity and coherence. Philosophers argue that utilitarianism can force someone to act in way that compromises their integrity. It could be argued that a strong wish to study Classical languages represents a kind of integrity which our education systems tend to compromise. Economic arguments reinforce the argument showing that Classical subjects are expensive with their small numbers. This can often be solved by combining classes, teaching off timetable and other devices which Classics teachers are only too willing to implement given the chance. The more inflexible centralised education systems find this solution more difficult to envisage, as they expect Classics to fit into the mould of everything else. Systems which allow more flexibility and autonomy to their teachers can provide more imaginative solutions to the problem of costs. At the level of costs of material and specialised equipment, however, Classical subjects are much cheaper to deliver than some other subjects. The comparison which emerges in the chapter from France between Classical subjects and threatened ecological species is worth examination (Denis-Laroque, this volume). If we are willing to take special measures to protect a butterfly, should we not also do the same for an ancient language which is one of the bases of our own civilisation and culture?

European Classics organisations

Contact has been maintained between teachers of Classics in the different European countries over the years and some conferences and publications have emerged from this. The *Colloquium Didacticum* performed this function for some time and has published papers from its congresses (Wülfing 1988, Matthiesen 1988, Decreus 2002). A new organisation came into being in 1990 which sought to unite in one federation all the national associations of Classics teachers. It is called Euroclassica. It holds an annual congress in a different European country each year, publishes a newsletter, and runs summer schools for students in Greece and Italy. Depending on the generosity of the country hosting the annual conference, the papers of this congress are sometimes published: those of the conference held in Chios, Greece, in 1997 under the title *Homer and European Literature* (Livadaras 2002) and those of the conference held in Coimbra, Portugal, in 2002 with the title *Penelope and Odysseus* (Oliveira 2003). Euroclassica is an excellent source for information on the national associations of each country. These associations are the powerhouses of Classics teaching for each nation state and are usually the first point of contact for every teacher. However, national associations are by their nature national, and are concerned first of all with what is happening in their own country. The intricacies of national examination systems and internal reforms will always be their primary focus, as will be clear from the accounts from each country.

However, on a European level there is much to be gained from cooperation and exchanging ideas, and this is the gap which Euroclassica aims to fill. Contacts are established, initiatives are started and projects are undertaken. It is true that Euroclassica has been unable to have any impact at the level of the European Union on education in Classical subjects, but this is because education is an area where the EU can have little direct input. This is a strictly national matter which the European Commission and the European Parliament tend to steer clear of and leave to national governments. One country's association (the French CNARELA) has preferred to remain outside the umbrella of Euroclassica and has felt that its energies are better directed towards its own internal concerns. Another (Italy) has no unifying single association and thus has been limited in the role it could play. Most countries, however, have remained supportive and have encouraged any initiatives that have been proposed. Those countries in Central and Eastern Europe which were for so long cut off from direct contact with the West have been among the most appreciative of this new network, although their small numbers and lack of resources have meant they have felt the demand for contributions more exacting. Others have been extraordinarily generous with their time and their hospitality during the meetings. In general the different associations have been glad to offer themselves for the annual meeting which has never had to revisit a location over the years of its existence.

Annual congresses have been held in the following places, after preliminary meetings in France and Denmark:

1993: Madrid, Spain
1994: Ambleside, UK
1995: Luxembourg
1996: Nijmegen, Netherlands
1997: Chios, Greece
1998: Heidelberg, Germany
1999: Prague, Czech Republic
2000: Brussels, Belgium
2001: Switzerland
2002: Coimbra, Portugal
2003: Vienna, Austria
2004: Genoa, Italy
2005: Dubrovnik, Croatia
2006: Uppsala, Sweden.

The list gives some idea of the variety of places which are willing to host a congress. Attention is currently turning towards various projects using new and traditional technology which are aimed at supporting colleagues throughout Europe in their teaching.

Euroclassica is a federation or umbrella organisation for all national associations. At the individual school level it has been unable to intervene. The European Union project Comenius is available for just such cooperation between schools. In 2004 my own school (European School Brussels1) joined a group of schools from Italy, Poland, the Czech Republic, Austria, Spain and Bulgaria who are all collaborating on *Latinità o Europa*. This kind of project is open to all schools within the EU but depends on the individual initiative of particular schools to get under way. Classical subjects are an excellent area in which schools from diverse parts of Europe can work together, and need not involve the Classics teachers exclusively. Others from humanities and modern language departments could equally participate. More information is available from www.latinitas.altervista.org.

Another parallel project, again with European Union backing, is the CIRCE project. CIRCE (Classics and ICT Resource Course for Europe) is a Comenius programme with the support of the European Commission which aims to set up a resource base in Classics for all teachers in Europe. It is publishing a manual of theoretical and practical tips with a bank of useful case studies; it has established a website (http://circe.cti.gr) which contains lesson plans and many resources for teachers; and finally it sets up and runs courses for teachers, training them in the use of ICT in teaching Classics.

Other conferences have been held to discuss and further cooperation between teachers of different European countries (Lister, forthcoming). Nearly all these projects use English as the lingua franca. The emergence of English as the preferred language of communication between the countries of Europe has, it must be admitted, also served to exclude francophone teachers from these exchanges of ideas and resources. It is a duty of European Classics teachers to reach out to those who prefer to use French as their first or second language of communication.

European Schools

These schools were set up to cater for the children of officials working for the European Union in ten different countries (Brussels with three schools and Mol in Belgium, Luxembourg, Varese in Italy, Culham in the UK, Karlsruhe, Munich and Frankfurt in Germany, Alicante in Spain, and Bergen in the Netherlands). These children are taught in language sections principally in their first language or mother tongue. Teachers are seconded by their national educational systems to teach their own subject to children from their own country in their first language, and also to teach children from the other countries in what is the pupils' second or third language. Thus English, for example, is taught as first language to those in the English-language section by UK or Irish teachers, but is also taught by the same teachers as second and third language to the pupils of the other language sections. History and Geography are taught to the

European Baccalaureate in the students' second language by native speakers using only the target language.

Latin is taught from the third year of secondary school (pupils aged about 13) as an optional subject. It can be chosen as an option right up to the European Baccalaureate at age 18. It is taught in the first language, that is to say the language of the section. Thus in my present school there are teachers of Latin from Denmark, France, Germany, Italy, Spain and the UK. We have recently been joined by teachers from Poland, Slovenia and Hungary. In the past I have also had colleagues from Greece and the Netherlands. I have taught Latin (through English) to pupils from France, Germany, Austria, the Netherlands, Italy and Slovenia as well as those from the UK and Ireland. Some of these I have taught to baccalaureate level and others to intermediate level. When a student from another country joins your class as a beginner, there is not much noticeable difference between him or her and the others, but when they join after some years of Latin in their own country, the variations of tradition, pronunciation, methodology and their expectations of what a Latin lesson should be, can be fascinating. There are frequent meetings and interchanges of ideas between the colleagues which can give rise to exchanges and experiments in methods. At one point the Cambridge Latin Course was being used by four different language sections. The English-language section used it as a base course book; the Danish used it occasionally as extra reading material; the Spanish used the Spanish-language version as their course book; and one Italian teacher was inspired by the favourable mention of it in Rossi (1996) to use it also as extra reading for the quality of the stories and to increase reading speed. (It was very firmly removed by his colleague, who disapproved of English entirely, the following year.)

Classics today

Because we have so thoroughly digested into our ways of thought the lessons that the ancient world has to teach us, it may be argued that we no longer need to have any acquaintance with these ideas at first hand. It is true to say that even if today's pupils in school do not have actual lessons in Classical Studies on their timetables they will nevertheless have to come to terms with Classics in some form or other: Classical forms of literature in their mother tongue and foreign language studies; technical Greco-Latin vocabulary in their science lessons; humanistic methodology in history and other arts subjects. Then later they may come across Oedipus in their Psychology lessons, Plato in their Philosophy classes, Tacitus in their Political Science; medical students will have to cope with terms that derive directly from Latin or Greek, law students will come across Roman Law and many Latin legal terms. They will have to take on board the debt that the texts they read owe to a Classical background: the debt of Hobbes to Thucydides, of Shakespeare to Ovid, of Machiavelli to

Livy, of Molière to Plautus, of Joyce to Homer, and so on. Given that they have to do this somewhere, there still should be a place for an introduction for everyone to the basics of all this at school. There must also be a place for centres of Classical Studies to keep our understanding of the ancient world up to date, so that the translations and accepted interpretations that the majority of us will use are constantly challenged and revised. University courses in some countries still seem to be continuing and even expanding, but they need a base of students on which to draw, though many are successfully attracting students who come new to Classics at undergraduate level.

This includes additionally (or even especially) those for whom Western civilisation is not their automatic cultural inheritance, that is those from non-European cultures and religions who now find themselves in the West having to cope with the unstated cultural assumptions of their European neighbours. Some education in the Classical inheritance is vital for them if they are to be able to understand the culture in which they live. It may be time to rediscover the contribution of Turkey, Egypt and the rest of North Africa to the Classical inheritance, which underpins Western culture. This may serve to give these young people from different backgrounds who now live in Europe a greater stake in European culture than they feel they have at present.

In *Antiquité et temps modernes, ou les changements dans les conditions de savoir* (in Decreus 2002) Freddy Decreus analyses two possible responses to the perceived crisis facing Classics today. One is to indulge in the 'culture of complaint' which seeks to lay the blame for the current situation at the feet of the students, their parents, society as a whole, new technology, or any other convenient scapegoat. Examples of this are to be found in *Who Killed Homer?* (Davis Hanson and Heath 1998). These authors blame the practitioners of Classical Studies in the universities themselves for the alleged decline. Allan Bloom's *The Closing of the American Mind* and other contributions to the 'culture wars' in the USA are examples of the same response, and Françoise Waquet's *Le Latin ou l'empire d'un signe* (Waquet 1998/2001) would also fall into this category.

On the other hand we can go with the flow and accept the changing position of all knowledge and attitudes towards literature and the established canon in a postmodern world (Beard 1995, Beard and Henderson 1995, Du Bois 2001). Decreus quotes the example of Greek Tragedy and its modern manifestations to show how this can be possible (see for example Hall, Macintosh and Wrigley 2004). By taking part in a public debate, showing a concern for contemporary problems through the means of Greek texts and facing up to such questions as gender issues and imperialist ambitions, Classical Studies can show that it is still part of the intellectual fabric of twenty-first-century life. This involves, says Decreus, admitting to ourselves that the old methods cannot be sufficient on their own to serve the cause of continuing Classical Studies: '*Nous, les philo-*

logues classiques, devons apprendre à interpréter le passé en fonction du présent et de l'avenir. Il est donc dangereux de nous limiter uniquement aux réflections qui ont déjà servi. ... La philosophie "back to basics" est donc insuffisante à elle seule à sauver l'héritage des classiques.' ('We Classics teachers must learn to interpret the past in terms of the present and the future. It is therefore dangerous to limit ourselves only to the reflections which have already served us. ... Thus the philosophy of "back to basics" is insufficient in itself to preserve the heritage of Classics.' Decreus 2002). He is talking about Classical Studies at university level and in Western cultural life generally, but there are ways in which these arguments affect Latin and Greek in schools too. Other contributors to *New Classics for a New Century?* (Decreus 2002) provide examples of the 'culture of blame' that Decreus himself analyses. For example, *'Ma famille est à l'image de la dégradation progressive des langues anciennes en France'* ('My own family is the image of the progressive decline of ancient languages in France', Martin 2002). Nascimento (for Portugal) provides an interesting discussion on the canon of Western literature and the part that schools must play in the preparation of students to read and make new interpretations of this agreed list of fundamental authors, in the face of all the questions posed to this idea by postmodernist criticism in general (Nascimento 2002).

USA

There is of course one important country missing from this volume. While not, of course, geographically in Europe, America maintains a tradition of Classics teaching. The state of Classics teaching in the USA has been excellently documented in the books of Richard LaFleur (most recently LaFleur 1998). The different contributors to this handbook of practice and methodology in USA Classics all show a deep commitment to the tradition of Classics, both in language learning (Latin and Greek) and in the wider civilisation and mythology courses which run in many schools and colleges. It appears there was a crisis in Classics in the 1970s when enrolments dropped dramatically during the atmosphere of reform and student unrest of the period. However LaFleur (1998) recounts a different story, where reform was embraced and with changing attitudes and methods the decline has been halted. The contributors tell of enthusiastic pupils and an impressive number of initiatives to motivate and retain students in Classics classes of all sorts. The decline in enrolments has not been reversed but has bottomed out and now remains steady.

Classical Studies are firmly called Latin and Greek in the USA and are included in all language programmes. Where there is an initiative to promote foreign language learning (particularly modern languages) Latin and Greek are always part of the package. There is a spirited debate over methods (grammar/translation as opposed to the reading approach), which is conducted without rancour. The connection between learning Latin and other foreign languages (particularly Spanish) is taken seriously and is seen by many to have a positive effect on language acquisition. There seems to be no distinction between types of institution (the public/private debate which particularly concerns the UK) and many of the contributions come from state schools. They recount initiatives which have been undertaken by teachers to suit their own situation in their individual schools or with specific groups of students, such as pupils with special needs. The Classics faculty of the USA appears from all this to be a confident and committed group of individuals who can even afford to have the occasional internal squabble. This can be seen in the argument over *Who Killed Homer?* (Davis Hanson and Heath 1998, Du Bois 2001), and in a situation where Classics is at the centre of the long-running debate over *Black Athena* (Bernal 1987). For those Europeans who are sceptical of America's attitude towards Europe there could be no better indication of the USA's historical links and commitment to basic European values than the state of Classics in American schools.

Conclusions

One of my Classics colleagues was talking to a group of other Classics teachers from a number of different countries. He said, in English (his second language), that he expected we would all agree that Classics was the basement of European civilisation. He is a good speaker of English but here he had grasped for a word and not quite got the right one. He meant something like foundation or basis. I was amused at first at the image of Classics being a kind of cellar or storeroom, but I remembered later that the metaphor had already been used by John Sharwood Smith in *On Teaching Classics* (Sharwood Smith 1977). There he compares Classics to an attic where a number of old artefacts and belongings are kept which are too valuable to throw away but not sufficiently in fashion to be taken out and kept in the living areas of the house. Nevertheless it is a fascinating place to rummage around in and find things you have forgotten about. Sometimes the objects will be difficult to interpret and will need specialised knowledge or research to understand fully. There, however, within the house is the whole history of the family and the culture it has lived in for a great number of years. We are at present busy putting a number of things away for storage, but as long as they stay tucked away, it will be possible for the next generation to find them there and to take them out, dust them off, and proudly present them to the members of the family as a piece of their past. When a piece is brought out from the attic and placed in a new context it can have a disconcertingly new effect and be seen in a totally fresh light. Some of us still like to go to the attic regularly so that we know what is there and can tell anyone who is interested where to find something. But there is still plenty of stuff there which has not been brought out for a long time. Instead of the attic many houses in continental Europe have capacious cellars or basements, possibly with lots of small areas which can be used as wine cellars or places to store things. They form the part of the house which holds the rest up and stores all its past history. Perhaps when we are considering the place of the study of ancient civilisations in the whole of Europe we should adapt Sharwood Smith's metaphor into a more European model and consider Classics as the basement in both senses of modern European education.

These chapters show that we have a lot to learn from each other. In some countries teachers may well feel they are in a position of permanent crisis; in others there may be a more stable situation. In some countries there are controversies over which approach to take to maintain the presence of Classics: traditional/progressive, rapid reading/grammatical knowledge, civilisation/language. In others teachers are more unified. Where the contribution indicates that there is neither an ongoing feeling of threat to the subject nor divisions among teachers over which approach to take, this may well indicate that things are generally satisfactory (or that the crisis is yet to come). Of course, the starting point for any crisis is going to be different in each case. A slight revision of the timetable provision from a solid base is far from a possible complete disappearance of Classics from all schools. As we tend to know only what is happening in our own country it is difficult to make an accurate judgement on how serious the situation is for another one. The contributions here may help us to begin to fill in the gaps and to provide a basis for future decisions. If we can understand and adapt for our own purposes the best characteristics and experiences of each country, we could present the best possible arguments and practices to those taking decisions which will affect the future of our subject. These seem to me to be: the deep commitment to their cultural heritage of the Italians and the Greeks; the energy and refusal to compromise over changes to the curriculum of the French; the seriousness of purpose and European awareness of the Germans; the ingenuity and innovations of the English; the quiet continuity of the Scandinavians who keep things going in systems without a long tradition; the courage of countries who have had to cope with governments who have been less than helpful to a free education; the willingness and even enthusiasm to adapt to new situations in Spain and Portugal; the ability of Belgium to withstand pressure and to adapt; and the commitment in the Netherlands to continue with the study of ancient civilisations and languages compulsorily at the university entrance level. I am certain more could be added.

Recent writers have shown from their researches that Classicists have always moaned about the state of their subject, claiming that things are getting worse, students are less able, and society is against them (Beard 1995, 2004; Stray 1998; Waquet 1998/2001). They argue that this goes to show that Classical Studies tend to continue in spite of everything that is thrown against them (although Waquet appears to believe that things really are getting worse and that the end is in sight). I recall a representative of the Catholic Church being interviewed by a journalist about some current crisis that was facing the Church. He was asked if this crisis would spell the end of the Church. He replied that the Catholic Church had seen the end of the Roman Empire, the Reformation, innumerable wars, the rise of science and atheism and many other setbacks, and yet had somehow managed to keep going. He did not think it needed to be too worried about this particular problem. Although Classics may not survive in exactly the same form that we are used to or even one which we would like, we should perhaps have more confidence in the ability of our subject to continue to have a presence in the future culture of Europe. And in the assurance that we have played a part in its long series of metamorphoses.

Austria

Alfred Reitermayer

History of Classics teaching

For centuries Classics teaching in Austria was highly influenced by Erasmus' heritage of preferring Latin to Greek and of dealing with Latin only for its grammar and style. Even in the twentieth century, *Liber Latinus*, a widely used Latin textbook with a highly regarded and clear traditional method of teaching Latin lexis and grammar, made generations of pupils see Latin sometimes as a drill or a factory for grammar.

In the late 1970s, influenced by the new approaches to course books in the UK, a new approach to Latin was made by *Via Nova*. This textbook allowed teachers to cut back to some extent on grammar teaching, focusing instead on reading continuous passages of Latin. The problem which pupils and teachers had with this kind of textbook was that the simultaneous appearance of the different declensions and conjugations – an attempt to make it possible to read interesting texts at the earliest possible moment – was hard for beginners, and sometimes harder for their parents who were trying to help them as they were used to learning Latin declensions and conjugations one after the other.

However, the controversy between traditional grammarians and 'new approach' or progressive teachers eventually resulted in three other new courses, *Veni Vidi Didici* (a mixture of traditional grammar with regular sections on Roman and Greek history and myths, Stockmann 2005), *Felix* which was replaced by *Prima* (Schüller 2005) in 2005/6 and *Ludus* (with simultaneous grammar and cultural sections, Kautzky and Hissek 2004). *Ludus brevis* (Widhalm-Kupferschmidt 2004) and *Medias in res!* (Hissek and Kautzky 2005) are short basic course books with a remarkable return to traditional transparent grammar lessons.

The modern secondary school system

Secondary schools in Austria generally admit pupils at age 10 and then put them through three distinct stages of education. Key Stage 1 takes students through years 5 to 6 with no special examination at the end and English beginning for all pupils at age 10. Key Stage 2 gives the pupils the opportunity to add Latin (the so-called *Long Latin*) with three hours per week for the first year and four hours per week in each year thereafter until year

12. Alternatively they can take another foreign language, usually French, Italian or Spanish, with the same time allocation until year 12. On the other hand they can opt for a type of school which does not teach a second foreign language, but which has more mathematics and natural sciences. Key Stage 2 takes students through years 7 to 8 and ends without a special examination. Key Stage 3 takes students through years 9 to 12.

Students can decide for *Short Latin* with three hours per week for four years, or Greek or *Short French* or, alternatively, Natural Science or Music and Arts or Information Technology. In year 10 these students opt for an extra four additional hours (two hours per week) for a language or another subject, which are called *Wahlpflichtgegenstände* (elected compulsory subjects). These are important for the type of final examination, called *Reifeprüfung*, in year 12. At the moment Latin is still a required subject for about 40 subjects at the university, even for studying Medicine and Law. The longer course of Latin is available only in Austrian grammar schools, but vocational schools provide a short course under the title *Freigegenstand*. At university level there are special courses called *Ergänzungskurse*.

Classical subjects within the secondary system

In 1987/8, 75,000 pupils attended Latin lessons and 2,400 took Greek lessons; in 2001/2, 53,000 pupils attended Latin lessons and nearly 1,000 took Greek lessons; in 2004/5, 64,000 attended Latin lessons and about 1,800 took Greek lessons.

Some favourable developments have been noted in 2003/4. Among these was a genuine interest taken in the position of our subjects by those politicians responsible for secondary education. A basic Latin module for all pupils from age 10 to 11 (two hours per week for two years) has been proposed. When the selection process of pupils by ability begins this programme should help distinguish those pupils who are suited to modern languages or Classics from those suited to natural sciences.

The most important development was the creation of a new curriculum for Latin and Greek for years 9 to 12 starting in autumn 2004. For the first time a special canon of authors is no longer compulsory but has been replaced by a canon of topics widespread over the centuries where Latin and Greek influenced history, architecture, arts, religion and rhetoric. More information on this can be found at www.lateinforum.at.

The essence of the future examination programme for year 12 in 2008/9 will be the fundamental harmony between its two halves, both the part for which the individual schools bear full responsibility with *Wahlpflichtgegenstände* and the part for which the examination papers are centrally prepared by a Government Board. The emphasis in the new system is on the literary value and the importance of the contents of the texts studied in the classroom.

How to become a teacher of Classics in Austria

The process is fairly well defined. Students leaving school will embark on a degree course in Classics and another subject at university, which will generally last three years. The qualification gained will usually be a Bachelor of Arts. After this course of study, students enrol on one or two years' further study, where they are provisionally awarded a *Magister Phil.* (qualified teacher status), which entitles them to teach in any Austrian school. They still face a period of one year, during which their professional qualities are scrutinised, before they are fully qualified.

Further information

Austria's vision and focus of effort in the next few years will be on implementing the first step of Euroclassica's European Curriculum in cooperation with politicians in some pilot grammar schools in Austria. There will be a pilot programme of two hours per week beginning at the age of 10; the goal is for Latin to become a compulsory subject for pupils at the age of 10, continuing until they are 11. After this compulsory humanistic basic module, a satisfactory classification into different types of grammar school according to a pupil's abilities will easily be made, because after two years of learning Latin it will be evident whether the pupil is a translating type or a communicative type or talented in natural science and mathematics. If the pupil is really talented in Latin then he or she should freely be able to choose a grammar school with Latin continuing for two hours per week and Greek beginning at the age of 13. Thus Latin can help to classify pupils according to their talents more effectively than now, and consequently we shall have the right pupils in the right types of grammar school, leading to less frustration for both pupils and teachers. Though this project has some support many teachers feel that two hours per week is not enough and view this programme as a diminution of the place of Latin in the curriculum.

There is further advice and information about this process at www.lateinforum.at

Belgium

I. FLANDERS

Joeri Facq and Liesbet Waumans

The history of teaching Classics

There are some studies on the evolution of education in Belgium, but so far little attention has been paid to the evolution of teaching Classics. Besides a few small and fragmentary articles there is no general overview on the way in which Classics teaching in secondary education has evolved during the past two centuries. There is still a lot of research to do and as yet not enough concrete information concerning this subject.

The modern secondary school system

During the past decades there have been four major state reforms (the first in 1970, the last in 1993), which have turned Belgium into a federal state with three communities: a Flemish-speaking, a French-speaking and a German-speaking community. Owing to these reforms education is no longer, as it used to be, the responsibility of the federal government, but is now the responsibility of the communities. Within this article we will restrict ourselves to the Flemish Community, which is a partner in the CIRCE project.

Compulsory education

Education in Flanders is compulsory. It starts on 1 September of the year in which a child reaches the age of six and lasts for 12 full school years. After six years of primary education a child goes to secondary school at the age of 12. Secondary education also lasts for six years, divided into three stages of two years. From the second stage onwards there are four types of secondary education: general, artistic, technical and vocational. In all types there are many different study disciplines from which a pupil can choose.

Educational networks

Both publicly and privately run education exists in Flanders. State education is organised by the Flemish Community, by the provinces or by the cities and municipalities. About 70% of all schools are privately run, and the majority of these are Catholic faith schools. These privately run schools are also subsidised by the Flemish Community. Although there may be some small differences among the four educational networks, the basic rules are imposed by the Flemish government. These basic rules concern the structure and the organisation of education (e.g. three stages, educational types, age of compulsory education, etc.) and the attainment targets (i.e. minimum objectives that should be aimed for and achieved by the majority of pupils).

Evaluation

There is no system of central examination. Every teacher is responsible for the assessment of his or her own pupils. Of course this does not mean that assessment is completely arbitrary. The attainment targets, the curricula and the educational guidance services provide the teachers with instructions and suggestions on how to evaluate. Two or three times a year (always before the Christmas and the summer holidays, in the first and second stages of privately run education, and mostly also before Easter) schools organise examinations, in which the material of the past months is tested.

Classical subjects within the secondary system

Latin

Pupils can study Latin from age 12 during the whole of secondary education, i.e. for six years. From the second year they can continue to study only Latin or they can combine it with Greek. In the third stage of secondary school there are four possible combinations: Latin and Greek, Latin and modern languages (French, English, German and Spanish), Latin and sciences (Biology, Chemistry and Physics) and Latin and Mathematics (with six or eight teaching periods of Maths a week). According to the educational network, the study discipline and the year, Latin is taught for four or five teaching periods of 50 minutes a week.

The first stage is principally dedicated to acquiring a foundation of Latin vocabulary and grammar; besides this, attention is paid to Classical culture and to reading (adapted) Latin texts. From the third year (or fourth at the latest) Latin authors are being read in their original form. There may be some differences among the educational networks, but on the curriculum in most schools are Caesar, Ovid, Virgil, Horace, Livy, Tacitus and Cicero; drama, Roman law and ancient philosophy are also compulsory.

Greek

Pupils can study Greek from the age of 13, starting in the second year of secondary education, i.e. for five years. They can choose to study only

Greek or they can combine it with Latin. In the third stage of secondary school there are three possible combinations: Greek and Latin, Greek and sciences (Biology, Chemistry and Physics) and Greek and Mathematics (with six or eight teaching periods of Maths a week). According to the educational network, the study discipline and the year, Greek is taught between two and five teaching periods of 50 minutes a week.

The teaching system for Greek is very similar to that for Latin. In the first two years (i.e. the second and third year of secondary education) most attention is paid to acquiring a foundation of vocabulary and grammar, but also to Greek history and culture and to reading (adapted) Greek texts. After that Greek authors are read in their original form. While state schools read these authors in a more thematic way (i.e. not by author, but by theme), in privately run education there is a kind of canon including, for example, Herodotus, Xenophon, Homer, the lyric poets, Demosthenes (or rhetoric in general), the tragedians and Plato.

Ancient Civilisation

In some schools in the privately run educational network there is a subject called Ancient Civilisation, which is taught for one teaching period a week. But normally the teaching of Classical history and culture is integrated in the lessons of Latin and Greek. The subject History (taught for two teaching periods a week) also dedicates a full school year in the first stage to the history of the ancient world (Egyptians, Greeks and Romans).

Some numbers

The total secondary school population in the Flemish Community consists of about 440,000 pupils. Nearly 75,000 of them follow education in the Flemish Community educational network (*Gemeenschapsonderwijs*), and of these about 16,000 pupils study Classics (Greek can count on the interest of only 800 pupils). Taking into account the other educational networks as well, there must be some 64,000 pupils studying Classics in secondary education (about 5,000 of whom choose to study Greek as well as Latin).

How to become a teacher of Classics

It is possible to study Latin at a higher level outside university. These studies last for three years and lead to a bachelor's degree. Such teachers can only work in the first stage of secondary education, but there are only a few of them. In this case the initial teacher training is part of the instruction. In practice nearly all Classics teachers have a master's degree. They have studied Latin and Greek at university for four years. Three Flemish universities offer Classical scholarship: Brussels, Ghent and Leuven. The main courses in these studies are Latin and Greek language and literature, ancient history, philosophy, religion and archaeology.

The initial teacher training for masters is also organised by universities. It consists of a one-year programme. The greater part of this teacher training is taken through more specific modules, with theory and practical exercises on teaching Classics. Students also have to do teaching practice in a secondary school. The way in which to apply for a job in education depends on the educational network. In the Flemish Community there is a kind of centralised system. The state schools are divided into 28 groups, and teachers must apply for a job in each school group. In privately run education a teacher normally applies directly to individual schools.

After practising for several years as a temporary teacher, a teacher may be able to become permanent if a vacant post becomes available. Unless the teacher is very fortunate, this temporary situation can last for many years before he or she can apply for a suitable position.

Evolution in Classics teaching

Learning plans in all educational systems now emphasise a 'functional approach' to grammar. This means that Latin and Greek are no longer taught with the sole objective of achieving a grammatical understanding of the Latin and Greek language system. It is now generally agreed that knowledge of grammar enables pupils to do nothing more than decipher authentic Latin and Greek texts, without acquiring an understanding of their social, cultural and historical context. This new approach involves a different way of teaching and especially of evaluating and assessing. Active knowledge of grammar is not necessary anymore. On the other hand it is very important that grammatical phenomena are always situated in a natural syntactical and semantic context. To support the pupils' reading process it is necessary to develop and put into practice a method or system of reading, which can be taught.

However, lesson observations show that most of the Classics teachers are still immersed in their traditional view on teaching Classics. Grammar still has a very central and important place. In the reading process translation is the usual method, in such a way that the pupils' understanding of the Latin and Greek texts in many cases proceeds rather from reading the Dutch translation, and not from reading the original sense of the source text.

Textbooks

In the state education system the teaching and learning concept is the reading of short and mostly adapted authentic texts. In the privately run education system synthetic texts are developed to support and exercise the grammar initiation in the first years.

There are various textbooks available for the language methods of the privately run schools. For the first and second stages especially they are regularly updated and each unit contains grammar and exercises, reading passages and culture. They pay more and more attention to the continuation of the Latin and Greek vocabulary into modern languages and to different aspects of Classical culture. Wide reading of the target languages, on the other hand, especially in the first grade, could be more frequent and receive more emphasis. Pupils start reading authentic texts in the fourth year. For Latin they start reading Caesar, and for Greek mostly Xenophon. These authors are regarded as the exemplary authors of classic Latin and Greek.

In the state education sector the textbooks are constructed in much the same way. They start with reading (slightly adapted) authentic texts, which requires a strictly adapted reading method. In the third stage teachers usually make their own teaching material by putting together the authors and themes of the curricula.

Further information

Bibliography and Internet links

A very good and systematic overview of the educational system in Flanders is the booklet *Education in Flanders*, which is a broad view of the Flemish educational landscape, published in 2001 by the Education Department of the Ministry of the Flemish Community. It can also be consulted on the web at http://onderwijs.vlaanderen.be/english

The Internet addresses of the Classics departments of the three Flemish universities that offer Classics are as follows:
Brussels: www.vub.ac.be/ofiches/latijngrieks.html
Ghent: www.flwi.ugent.be
Leuven: http://millennium.arts.kuleuven.ac.be/klassiekestudies

The aims of the Flemish Classics Teachers' Association (*Vereniging van Leerkrachten Oude Talen*) are to promote the interest in Classical languages and culture, to improve the quality of Classics education, to support the Classics teachers and to defend their interests. Its website is www.vlot-vzw.be

II. FRENCH-SPEAKING BELGIUM

Fabienne Paternotte, Colette Goedert, Catherine Brux and Noëlle Hanegreefs (translated by John Bulwer)

Education is organised in Belgium by the different independent communities. There are considerable variations between them. Apart from

French-speaking education there is also a Flemish- or Dutch-speaking education system (see above), and a German-speaking one (though only a minority of pupils study in this last one.)

There are three different ways in which education is delivered in the French-speaking areas of Belgium. First there is the official education which takes place within the French Community. Then there is the official education of the cities, provinces and communes. Finally there is a system of free education, which is delivered in faith schools, either Catholic or non-denominational. All three are subsidised by the state. Although they have a certain degree of freedom, the three French-speaking systems generally maintain equivalent programmes of study.

In Belgium a teacher of ancient languages (*l'enseignant en langues anciennes*) signifies a person who teaches Latin and Greek in a secondary school. He or she has an official position which allows him or her to teach lessons of Latin and Greek as a priority. However, it can happen that such a teacher, when necessary, may be asked also to teach French as first language, History or Religion or Ethics, which may include an introduction to philosophy.

Teaching structure

Given the diversity within the different education systems in French-speaking Belgium, the number of hours for teaching Latin and Greek is variable. It also varies according to the cycles of education. There are three degrees or cycles: First cycle (12 to 13 years), Second (14 to 15) and Third (16 to 17). The following table shows the situation:

		Official education in the French community	*Official education in the cities, provinces and communes*	*Free (religious) education*
1st degree	Latin	4 hours	2-4 hours	2-4 hours
	Greek			1 or 2 hours
2nd degree	Latin	4 hours	4 hours	4 hours
	Greek	2-4 hours	3 or 4 hours	2 or 4 hours
3rd degree	Latin	4 hours	4 hours	4 hours
	Greek	2-4 hours	4 hours	2-4 hours

Only the Classical languages are taught. There is no longer a place for medieval or Neo-Latin in the current curriculum. Neither is there room for the teaching of Modern Greek. However, the new programmes of study encourage teachers to use language exercises which draw out the parallels between Ancient and Modern Greek.

The pronunciation generally used is the restored or Ciceronian pronunciation (*pronuntiatio restituta*). For Greek the Erasmian pronunciation is used throughout.

The place of the ancient languages in the modern world

The study and teaching of the ideas and the culture of the ancient world are designed to lead to a reflection upon our own age and current concerns.

There is no division between learning ancient languages and ancient civilisations. Learning the language leads to a more precise and sophisticated appreciation of the particular ancient culture. All language courses have a double aspect: language and civilisation.

The view of the public

Political decisions have modified the place of ancient languages in the school curriculum. Latin as well as Greek is now an optional course throughout secondary school and as a consequence there has been competition between the options; this has become all the more fierce given that the number of weekly hours is limited. Every year teachers of ancient languages have to fight to keep the number of hours which they have struggled to achieve. Nonetheless, access to the ancient languages is available to all.

Parents are generally in favour of the study of ancient languages, as they consider it a guarantee of a good level of education. The pupils themselves regard the subject in three ways: those who are not interested at all and who choose other options; those who take ancient languages under instructions from their parents; and finally those who take a genuine interest themselves in the subject. It would be difficult to comment on the interest of the media, as this depends on the type of media, the government and the current news.

The place of the ancient languages at school

The number of pupils choosing to study ancient languages is different in each of the educational systems. In the second and third degrees (pupils between 14 and 17 years old) in 2003/4 in the French-speaking education system, 4,105 pupils took Greek in either the two-period or the four-period course; and 24,104 pupils took Latin at four periods per week. To these figures can be added the many pupils who follow Latin in the first degree (12 to 14 years). However, it is difficult to give a precise number for these because of the variations between one school and another. It should be noted here that the place of the Classical languages remains fragile for pupils in the first degree because at this level they do not qualify as subjects for the certifying examination (*examen certificatif*) that the pupil must pass in order to qualify for the following year. (Passage to the following year for all pupils is dependent on success in these examinations.) In the other degrees, including the final year of school, the pupils are assessed at the end of each school year by examinations organised by each school. In general pupils are assessed in the following areas: grammar, translation with justifications, interpretation and vocabulary. They can be assessed by either written or oral examinations in the final years of their school career.

Classical studies are regarded as having an interdisciplinary effect which aids the pupil to succeed in further studies generally. The study of Latin and Greek seems to facilitate the learning of the linguistic structures and vocabulary of other languages taught in Belgian schools which are sometimes very different from French or Dutch (and German in the east of the country). Pupils have the chance to learn English, Spanish and Italian as well as other languages. Teachers firmly hold the opinion that, in common with other subjects, learning Latin and/or Greek can also develop a sense of logic and of reasoning and can exercise the memory.

The place of ancient languages at university

The French-speaking universities in Belgium (the Catholic University of Louvain, the Free University of Brussels and the University of Liège) all offer, since September 2004, a bachelor's degree in Ancient Languages and Literature which can be followed by a master's.

Special measures

Any additional help given to pupils to catch up or begin ancient languages later is left to the free choice of each school which can devote some of its timetable credits to this. There are, on the other hand, no summer schools for the learning of ancient languages. However, there are some summer courses for students wishing to take up courses in Classical Studies or who need to learn the languages for other types of study (Romance Philology, Ancient History, Oriental Studies and others).

Extracurricular activities

Teachers employ a whole range of activities to supplement their lessons: visits to theatres, to museums and to special exhibitions, and use of new media. All these as well as the lessons themselves can influence the pupils to continue in their choices. One small studio theatre in Brussels (Théâtre-Poème) offers regular performances of shows designed around a choice of texts from Latin and Greek authors. They do a dramatisation of the *Catilinarian Conspiracy*, for example, using extracts from Cicero's speeches and from Sallust. They offer another set of tales from Ovid's *Metamorphoses*, simple but effectively acted out. These are aimed at school audiences but also attract houses of the general public who seem to be familiar with subject matter, perhaps from their own schooldays.

Textbooks

The choice of textbook depends largely on the education system where the teacher concerned works. Official education usually makes use of the collection *Lux* (published by Dessain) for Latin teaching. In the Free Education sector the collection *Lavency* (published by De Boeck) is popular for Latin teaching. For Greek the most used collection is *Bourgaux* (published by Dessain).

The principle for the majority of textbooks used in Belgium is the following: pupils are exposed immediately to authentic texts, sometimes lightly adapted if the need is felt. Texts studied at the beginning of a Latin course are short texts (proverbs or fables of Phaedrus). Later, at an appropriate moment, attention is turned towards the study of authors (Caesar, Livy, Virgil, Cicero, Tacitus and others), sometimes in the form of selected extracts, sometimes through the intensive study of a particular work. In Greek the same pattern is adopted. Pupils begin with texts linked to certain sites in Greece, or with myths and historical episodes. Xenophon, Homer and Demosthenes are among the authors studied.

The rapid-reading approach to language is only rarely practised in Belgium. Basic grammar is studied by means of texts, which are authentic as far as possible. Etymological exercises are used to deepen the knowledge of the pupils' mother tongue. The textbooks are written in French and are relatively recent, dating from no more than 15 years ago and regularly updated. In the upper secondary school the pupils have gone beyond textbooks and need to read authors in their original texts. However, many old school editions of authors commonly read in school have disappeared and are no longer available. The ancient languages form part of the cultural heritage of Europe. This European aspect is emphasised in the choice of texts as well as by their interpretation and by illustrations.

The association of teachers of Classical languages in French-speaking Belgium is the *Fédération des professeurs de Latin et de Grec*, (www.fpgl.be). This organisation is always ready to resist changes to the status of Classics in the curriculum (Centre Jean Gol 2005) and arranges a regular programme of events, talks and activities to promote the study of Classics in all its aspects among the schools and general public.

Croatia

Zlatko Šešelj

Brief introduction – Classics in context

The situation in current Classics teaching in Croatia is a result of the cultural, political and also geographical circumstances of this region. Croatia occupies the area of Illyricum, the area that came under Roman rule in the middle of the second century BCE. After the breakdown of the Illyric rebellion in the year 3 CE (when the Romans were led by the future emperor Tiberius), the entire area quickly succumbed to Roman influence. Many places still provide evidence of this Roman presence, for example the Arena (amphitheatre) in Pula and Diocletian's palace in Split – to name only the most famous. In addition, the citizens of Poreč (Roman Parentium) still walk the Roman *decumanus*, which even continues to bear the same name. Taking a further step back into the past, there are still traces even of the ancient Greek world on the Adriatic coast of Southern Croatia: from the island of Mljet (Greek *Melitta*) – Calypso's mythical island of Ogygia – to the island of Hvar (Greek *Pharos*), whose surrounding fields are still divided by the boundaries created in the fourth century BCE. The earliest traces of written language in this area are indeed Greek. It can be seen that Greek civilisation persisted in this area even after the fall of the Western Roman Empire, so the barbarian Slavic tribes were to become neighbours to the cities and the rule of the Byzantine Empire (and were partly subdued by them).

Overshadowed by the Byzantine Empire, which drew on the Roman political and legal system, a young and small Croatian state was formed. In the tenth century, as the Byzantine presence in the Adriatic diminished, the Croatian kings took control of the entire eastern coast of the Adriatic and, under the influence of the mighty Order of St Benedict, accepted Latin as the formal language for political, religious and cultural communication and correspondence. When the Hungarian ruling dynasty inherited the Croatian crown (in the early twelfth century), and later when the Habsburg dynasty of Austria was elected in the early sixteenth century to bear the Croatian crown, Latin was the official language of the Croatian *Sabor* (parliament), and remained so until 1847. Thus Latin was the key element in preserving Croatian political identity (as opposed to Hungarian and German). From the Middle Ages, and almost to this day, numerous Croatian writers wrote in Latin – Marko Marulić from Split

(Marcus Marulus Spalatensis, the renowned fifteenth-/sixteenth-century author) being the most famous, and one who was frequently printed and read all over Europe. Some believe that the opus of the Croatian writers writing in Latin was second in size only to that of Italy. Bibliographic research (which has not yet been completed) has shown that there were more than 5,000 such authors. A huge literary heritage in Latin, as well as the ever present evidence of the ancient world in contemporary surroundings, brings the Classical world close to the minds of the Croatian people.

Classics teaching – historical introduction

Classics teaching in Croatia started, as elsewhere in Europe, under the influence of the Catholic Church. It gained momentum in the beginning of the seventeenth century, when the Jesuits founded many high schools in the country, starting with one in Zagreb in 1607, which has continued its mission without interruption until today, but with the name *Klasična gimnazija u Zagrebu* (*Gymnasium Classicum Zagrabiense*) since 1850. Jesuit high schools were based on the late classical principles of *trivium* and *quadrivium*. Encouraged by the success of the Zagreb school, the University of Zagreb (*Universitas Studiorum Zagrabiensis*) was founded in 1666 and the *Nacionalna i sveučilišna knjižica* (National and University Library) was founded at around the same time. With the 1850 school reform throughout the entire Austrian Empire (and thus in Croatia as well) a modern educational system was created. It assumed two types of schools: 'classical' high schools which led on to university and 'real' high schools that led only to higher education in the technical domain. In the 'real' school, the curriculum has always included a number of so-called 'real' subjects, such as Mathematics and Physics, but the 'classical' high schools, on the other hand, only introduced Mathematics as an optional subject at the very end of the nineteenth century! Latin (no longer the language of instruction) and Greek were taught in both types of school, but in 'real' high schools their scope was narrower and of shorter duration. These differences between the two types of schools are still present today, particularly in the field of Classics.

The situation today – timetables and subjects

Elementary and high school level

Classics are taught in Croatia in three different ways. First, continuing the tradition of the 'classical' education, Latin and Greek are taught alongside each other as a single unit, which continues to be a matter of significant debate. The attempts to diminish the role and importance of Classical Greek have been successfully rejected. In this model of Classics teaching, one option is to start learning Latin at the age of ten, and continue for eight years. Greek is taught from the age of 12 and continued for six years. It is unfortunate, however, that this option exists only in Zagreb. The other option is to start learning both Latin and Greek in high school (four years long) at 15 years of age, and to continue for four years. During this option, the content of instruction is divided into two phases: the first phase teaches the basics of Latin and Greek grammar and civilisation, while the second phase is devoted to extensive reading of authentic works of Classical literature, with emphasis on political and cultural aspects of the Classical world, such as philosophy, arts, science and the way of life. In this model either Latin or Greek must be included in the final examination.

Secondly, following the tradition of the so-called 'real' high schools, Latin is taught as a compulsory subject in all high schools, but is taught for two years only (from the start of high school education) at 15 and 16 years of age. Unfortunately, in those schools Greek has completely disappeared as a subject, while Latin can still be taken as an optional subject in the final two years, at the ages of 17 and 18. In this model, the content of the Latin syllabus comprises only the basics of Latin grammar and Roman civilisation.

Thirdly and finally, in certain schools of professional education, such as schools of nursing and veterinary medicine, Latin is taught as a necessary requirement for the vocational course under study. Its content comprises only the very basic grammar with a special emphasis on the relevant medical and biological terms and expressions, and possibly some basics of Classical civilisation.

The first model described above is taught in only 12 schools, nine of which are affiliated to the Catholic Church (although it is not intended solely for future clergy, but mainly for ordinary citizens), and two of which are public (one of them, *Klasična gimnazija*, I have already mentioned) and one private. All of them follow the state-approved curriculum, currently enrolling around 2,800 pupils. The second model comprises 60 high schools and around 23,000 pupils. The final model enrols around 5,900 pupils.

University level

Latin and Greek are taught at the University of Zagreb and the University of Zadar in the Classical Philology departments. Latin only can be studied at a number of other schools as well, such as the University of Rijeka. In Zagreb and Zadar around ten students a year enrol to study both Latin and Greek together, and around 80 students enrol to study either one or the other. Most students choose courses that will enable them to teach in schools, such as Didactics. At this university level, students have mandatory courses in Ancient History and are encouraged to take optional courses in Philosophy, Epigraphy and Linguistics. Students who have studied (and graduated in) Latin and Greek can teach only those subjects, and the knowledge they have gained through optional courses is used primarily to expand and enrich their syllabus when teaching. Students who have studied either Latin or Greek with another subject, such as History, Philosophy or Italian, can naturally teach both or either one of these. There is a very small number of students who decide to take up a particularly heavy workload by studying both Latin and Greek along with another subject, usually Archaeology or History.

Ancient Greek – Modern Greek

For 20 years already, Modern Greek has been a mandatory course for Greek majors at the University of Zagreb, and recently basic training in Modern Greek has become available at two high schools in Zagreb (*Klasična gimnazija* and *Privatna klasična gimnazija*).

Classical Studies or Classical Civilisation

At the elementary and high school education level, language courses include lessons about both Greek and Roman civilisation. Classical history, art, science and literature are included in various compulsory subjects such as History, Philosophy, History of Art, Sociology, Logic and History of Music. At university level there is no specific subject or field of study that could be called 'Classical Civilisation', but aspects of it are included in numerous courses from various different departments, most notably Archaeology, History, History of Art and Philosophy.

Extracurricular activities

The influence of Classical civilisation is strongly present in extracurricular activities, especially in elementary schools and high schools, and to a lesser degree at the universities. The most distinct of these activities are drama groups, which annually stage classical plays and take active parts in cultural displays. The most prominent of schools in this area is the *Klasična gimnazija* in Zagreb, which has continuously staged a Classical drama (tragedy or comedy) every year for over 50 years, and which has also had a regular performance at the Festival of Classical Theatre in Segóbriga, Spain, since 1995. In towns and cities where the history stretches as far back as the ancient Greek or Roman period, there are many archaeological monuments, parks and museums. Students and professional actors often work together to bring these sites to life by staging scenes from Classical history.

There are also a number of summer schools and seminars (on the island of Hvar, which was the Greek *Pharos*; at Salona, the capital of the Roman *Provincia Dalmatia*, near Split; and at Dubrovnik), as well as international seminars that Croatian students are invited to attend (including the Euroclassica summer schools in Athens and Chios and others).

Since 1987 an annual competition in Greek and Latin language has been held at both elementary and high school level. Candidates sit first a school competition, and then a local one, which leads to a provincial and finally a state competition. More than 100 students in six different categories reach the finals. Our students also take part in the international competitions, such as the *Certamen Ciceronianum Arpinas* at Arpino, Italy, and the International Competition in Classical Greek.

Given the proximity of Croatia to Greece and Italy, a great number of students are able to take trips to Rome and Greece. Students from Classical high schools regularly take their senior trip to either one of these destinations. A typical school trip to Greece would include visits to Olympia, Mycenae, Epidauros, Athens, Delphi and Sounion, and some trips might also include Crete and other Greek islands. Classical school trips to Italy would stop in Rome, Pompeii, Ostia, Villa Hadriana in Tivoli, and possibly Naples, the Etruscan settlements and the island of Sicily as well. College seniors usually coordinate trips throughout Italy, Greece and also Turkey, which is not yet an option in high school.

Textbooks

There are two levels of studying Latin or Greek – basic and advanced, both of which involve reading Classical literature. Textbooks in their usual form are primarily intended for the more basic level of instruction; there are five different textbooks for basic Latin and three for basic Greek. Original texts in Latin and Greek selected *in usum scholarium* are compiled in various *Anthologiae* and *Chrestomathiae*. Those books follow the usual canon of authors (Caesar, Cicero, Sallust, Nepos, Livy, Petronius, Suetonius, Tacitus; Virgil, Horace, Ovid, Catullus, Martial, Juvenal, Plautus; Xenophon, Herodotus, Demosthenes; Homer, Sappho, Alcaeus, Tyrtaeus, Mimnermus, Archilochus, Sophocles, Aeschylus, Euripides; Plato, Democritus, Heraclitus). A recent innovation has been to include certain Croatian Latinists, such as Marko Marulić (Marcus Marulus Spalatensis), Ivan Česmički (Janus Pannonius) and Antun Vrančić (Antonius Verantius) in the Latin reading programme.

Two publishers engage in the systematic publishing of Classical texts. The first is *Matica Hrvatska*, which started in 1880, and has since published a series of Croatian translations (around 50 titles). The *Bibliotheca Latina & Graeca* started in 1979, and has so far published approximately 50 titles both in the original language and in Croatian translation. Both publishers continue with their efforts. Other publishing companies (the most active being the publisher Demetra) also publish Classical authors, especially the works of philosophers. Literature in the field of Classical Studies is also published mostly by the companies mentioned above, but also by others such as *Školska knjiga*, *Profil*, *ArtTresor* and *Izdanja Antibarbarus*. The *Bibliotheca Latina & Graeca* evolved from the journal *Latina et Graeca*, which started in 1973. Recently there has been an increase in the demand for Neo-Latin texts and authors, and the publishers most engaged in this matter, among others, include the *Croatian Academy of Art and Science* and *Književni Krug Split*. Great attention has been devoted to Marko Marulić, whose work *De institutione bene beateque vivendi* was a European bestseller at the time.

Teacher training

Latin and Greek teachers have usually studied at the University of Zagreb, Zadar or Rijeka. Teaching experience is gained through theoretical courses and practical teaching while at university. The Croatian Association of Classical Philologists (*Hrvatsko društvo klasičnih filologa*), established in 1973, is most actively engaged in the continuing professional education of its Classics teachers. In the 20 years of its existence, the Association has organised numerous seminars, lectures, colloquia, symposia and educational trips for teachers and other members. It also publishes its bulletin *Nuntius*.

The media and the public

Classical topics constantly appear in the Croatian media, and are usually triggered by archaeological excavations or other discoveries of lesser or greater importance. The latter include the relatively recent discoveries of Lysippus's *Apoxyomenos* in the sea near the island of Lošinj, an amphitheatre from the Flavian era in the Roman *castrum Burnum*, and a group of imperial statues from the Roman city *Narona*, which were recently exhibited at the Ashmolean Museum in Oxford. Media coverage is devoted to festivals, anniversaries and other events related to Classical civilisation, both in Croatia and other countries. However, most experts agree that such cultural resources are not presented in an adequate and systematic way, which would help make them become more popular and more prominent among the general public. The same applies to various forms of popular science, where coverage could still be improved. It must be noted, however, that the Croatian general public is fond of and cares about its rich Classical heritage, and treats it with interest and respect. If it were not so, the foundations for studying Classics would be profoundly shaken. Fortunately, there is still great interest in studying Latin and Greek, and it is slowly becoming even more popular. More and more people recognise the value of learning Latin and Greek, primarily as a good stepping stone for broad education, and furthermore as an aid in studying modern languages. Until recently there still existed the belief that learning Classics was reserved only for the social elite. However, it is clear that those who have received an education which includes Classics in some form are not part of a *social* elite, but could certainly claim to be part of a *cultural* elite.

Czech Republic

Barbara Pokorná

Classical studies have had a long and deep tradition in the Czech Republic. There was a strong effort to keep the subject going even through the difficult years of communism. Indeed, Latin and Greek were perceived as rather undesirable not long ago, but a new interest in Classical education showed a general growth after 1989. New universities with departments focusing on ancient history and culture were established and the departments of Classical languages, which were abolished at the time of the general dissolution of humanities in the 1950s, were restored. However, the original enhanced interest dropped after several years and currently Classical languages are again fighting to gain ground in the curriculum of high schools and secondary schools.

Czech Classics teachers

The social status and public appreciation of teachers – particularly teachers of Latin and Greek – are very low in our country and do not correspond with the depth of their education and knowledge. It is assumed that a Classical Philologist is capable of reading and translating Latin and Greek texts, and that he or she has background education in not only ancient history, archaeology, literature, philosophy and art, but also in general linguistics. Despite this rich and wide knowledge the Czech Latin or Greek teachers have very limited prospects to apply that knowledge and learning. Owing to the very small allocation of hours – in the case where Latin and Greek are being taught at all at a school – they are forced to narrow down what they read and confine themselves to introducing the students to basic Latin (and rarely Greek) grammar. The majority of Latin and Greek teachers took their degrees not only in Classical Philology but also in another philological field, for example in a living language or Czech mother tongue or history. It is this second field which provides in most cases their main workload.

Course contents

The contents of the Latin course are affected by the time allowance given by a respective class allocation. For Latin it is usually two hours a week for two years. Students are instructed in the basics of Latin grammar, but in addition they are introduced to other areas such as ancient geography, politics and history, mythology, literature and art, through exposure to visual material and other more wide-ranging texts. Some schools with an extensive teaching of Classical languages refer to the rich tradition of medieval Latin and also humanistic and baroque literature, and in this way draw attention to the basic differences in vocabulary, morphology and syntax. As a result of this context, medieval Latin pronunciation is often used. (Greek is taught only very rarely at high schools, and these are mostly Classical and Episcopal secondary schools.)

Modern world

Several teachers, who deal with the pedagogical and didactic aspects of Classics teaching, often ask themselves how best to confront the Classical disciplines with the stormy development of the modern world, and how to make twenty-first century students interested in Latin and Greek. There is a wide choice of well-established arguments, proven over time, namely those relating to European roots, cultural heritage or a basis for foreign languages. To keep up with the pace of modern life, the students are addressed in the books especially by concrete connections and analogies to our current world, by cyclically repeated situations and problems in the history of mankind. The reception of Greek and Roman history, mythology and literature in current writings, theatre, film, music or visual arts has the opportunity to bring to life a culture which is thousands of years old. In addition attention is drawn to the technical terminology used in the fields of law (condition *sine qua non*), medicine (*sub signo veneni*), natural sciences (*coccinella septenpunctata*) and linguistics (*nominativus*), and also to such everyday terms as audio, video, computer, delete, etc. in order to give evidence of the dynamics of a seemingly 'dead' language.

Language and civilisation

For many decades Classical Studies have been perceived in our country as a linguistic domain and the discussions on their wider conception are gaining ground only now. As a result, though Classical Philologists are indeed educated in all related disciplines, they are in reality obliged to focus their attention mostly on Latin grammar. The most urgent requirement for such a new concept of teaching and of the introduction of courses on ancient civilisation would be first of all new modern textbooks, which Czech teachers currently lack.

Timetable and curriculum

Students of Czech secondary schools begin learning Latin between the ages of 15 and 17. Greek is taught only rarely and at only a few Classical and Episcopal secondary schools, whose total number does not exceed ten. The individual curricula vary according to each school, and as Latin is only an optional course it is always up to the director of the school to determine whether it will be covered or not. The time allocation is mostly two hours per week for two years, sometimes less and seldom more. The only nation-wide Latin examination at secondary schools is the school-leaving examination – if the student opts for it. It is principally for students who plan to study Classical Philology at the university level.

Politics

Teaching Latin and Greek is on the margin of interest in the Czech Republic, and thus also outside politicians' concern. These domains are in a way considered elite and beyond the average level of achievement, because the present educational trends are based on a pragmatic approach, which does not correspond with the nature of Classical languages. It is thought that their practical use cannot be exactly defined. Therefore, we find that the only students who are interested are those whose parents learnt Latin, or who plan to utilise it in their further education. The permanent interest of such students makes a significant counterbalance to technical fields and to natural science.

Media

Not even the media dedicate much attention to Latin. An exception was the successful TV Latin course *Disco Latine* broadcast several years ago. Nevertheless, we meet ancient culture indirectly in the media via documentaries, travelogues, TV contests, and also quotations – unfortunately with inevitable errors.

Modern languages

One of the traditional arguments supporting Classical languages is that learning Latin (and Greek) makes it easier to learn other modern living languages. However, Czech teachers often use this argument the other way round. Students come to the Latin classes with a knowledge of another language (most often it is English, German, Spanish or French) in order to understand its Latin or Greek origin in lexicology, morphology and even syntax.

Universities

The situation at our universities has improved markedly since 1989, but the Classics departments have been struggling with a lack of students in the past few years. That is caused by a relative lack of opportunities to study Latin or Greek at secondary schools and so here we start to move in an ever smaller vicious circle – Classical languages are not being taught at secondary schools, with the result that students choose not to study them at universities. There are departments of Classical Languages only at the universities in Prague, Brno and Olomouc, but Latin, and alternatively Greek, are also taught at a number of departments of Philosophy, and also at faculties of Medicine, Law, Theology and even Physical Education.

Outside the school environment, students do not have many opportunities to meet with ancient culture and Classical languages. Language schools do not teach Latin or Greek, and school trips to discover ancient monuments are not a common practice at secondary schools. Thus, if a student is truly interested, almost the only possibility is to see ancient theatre plays and films and to read ancient literature. Every year the Association of Teachers of Classical Languages (ALFA), in cooperation with the Institute of Classical Studies in Prague, organises a summer school of Classical Studies, in which both teachers and students can participate. The Association programme also comprises international visits. A website is under construction, and the periodical *Echo Latina* has finished a short run of publication.

Textbooks

A high-quality, modern and attractive textbook is considered one of the most important preconditions for a successful course. Such a textbook, with the basis of a simple grammar explanation, allows a prompt understanding of original texts. Czech textbooks usually build on a long tradition of grammar (e.g. Španár and Kettner, *Latina pro gymnázia*, 1991; Pech, *Latina pro gymnázia I*, 1998; Pros, *Latinitas viva I, II*, 1998). They systematically familiarise the students with basic Latin grammar, which allows them to translate first of all synthetic texts and further on parts of authentic texts, quotations and sayings. The most commonly translated authors are Caesar, Ovid, Cicero, Tacitus and Catullus, and from non-classical writings the most widely read are, for example, *Carmina Burana* and *Gaudeamus igitur*.

Grammar instruction plays a primary role in the Latin courses taught at the Czech secondary schools. It consumes 80% of the allocated time. Instruction concentrated on history, literature, geography, politics or art and culture is only an optional supplement to classwork owing to time restrictions. So far Czech teachers lack a textbook which would resemble a child's box of bricks, combining language instruction with elements of ancient civilisation. Experienced teachers include etymological references in their course, which enable the students to understand technical terminology and foreign languages in greater depth.

It follows from what has been said that in our country the term 'Classics' has ceased to be a strictly defined term. It has concrete outlines and contents only for teachers and scholars dealing with the ancient world. Still, the present vagueness of the term might be an advantage for us. In light of the recent entry of the Czech Republic into the European Union in 2004, we might soon become able to give the term Classics the attribute *European* again. Although Classics teachers in the Czech Republic are very few in number and are active at present in only a few schools, they hope that Classics will begin to have a more meaningful significance to a people who are able once again to rejoin the rest of European culture from which they were divided for so long.

Denmark

Elisabeth Nedergaard

Prologue

Latin, Greek and Hebrew used to be the three main subjects to be learned in school in Denmark, marking the three principal pillars of European culture: the Greek, the Roman and the Christian. That was back in the schooldays of the Danish philosopher Søren Kierkegaard (1813-55) whose life and work indeed reflect his education at school. Much has changed since. Society has changed. The economic basis of society has developed from agriculture through industry to modern technology. Christianity is in serious decline and is no longer the only religion to be considered in the new multi-ethnic society. Where upper secondary education and university studies in the nineteenth century were for the chosen few, *lifelong education* has now become the key phrase for all members of society. The education system has followed the development of society with a series of reforms, the latest of which has been implemented from the beginning of the school year 2005/6. We continue to be in a period of transition.

Classics after the reform of 2005

In the school system that we are leaving, the upper secondary school was divided into two major branches: Languages and Science. This division disappears with the new reform. At the same time, Latin as a compulsory subject (C-level, one year) also disappears. In the old system, this was taught for all language students (aged 16 to17) with three lessons a week for the first year, after which Latin would become optional at either A-level (two more years) or B-level (one more year). Science students of the old system could choose Latin as an optional one-year C-level, but only a few students did so.

In the new system, compulsory Latin will be replaced by a new collaborative subject called *Almen Sprogforstaaelse* (General Linguistics). This subject covers about 45 hours of the first half-year of the general upper secondary education. The subject is to be taught in collaboration by the teachers of Danish and the teachers of foreign languages, among them Latin. The Latin part of General Linguistics will normally cover about half of the course. The students are not supposed to learn to read Latin for Latin's own sake in 15 to 20 hours, but they are to be introduced to various important aspects of Latin, especially concerning the impact of Latin on modern foreign languages. The number of lessons to be assigned to the Latin part of the General Linguistics course is not static, however. Each school has to decide on a distribution of the 45 lessons in total on the various subjects involved. This means that the Latin teachers in some schools have to fight with their own colleagues to get the number of lessons needed to meet the conditions prescribed by the Ministry of Education. This is a very unpleasant situation for those involved.

With the reform, Latin as a compulsory C-level disappears and the B-level will no longer be an option, but the A-level will continue to exist in a few schools, depending naturally on whether the students choose to have it or not. In most of the Latin A-level schools, the Latin A-level will be combined with an A-level in Ancient Greek as well. With the new reform, the students will have to choose which subjects to have as main subjects by the time they leave public school (at age 16) and enter the *Gymnasium* (the last three years of their school education). Latin is rarely taught in public schools and the students will have no real background for choosing Classics with the new reform. In the old system for the general upper secondary education, the students would choose their main subjects only after the first year of the *Gymnasium*. In the old system, only about 100 students graduated with A-level Ancient Greek and about 225 with A-level Latin. There is a good reason to be worried for the future of A-level Classics in the system to come.

One can hope that the General Linguistics course will capture the interest of some students so much that they will want to add an optional C-level of Latin (or Ancient Greek) to their education. In that case, this will not be one of the core subjects in the student's education. The one-year free optional C-level Latin (or – more rarely – Ancient Greek) will be an open option for most students no matter what core subjects they may have chosen. Most students, however, will have room for only one free optional subject, so competition will be hard with many other interesting possibilities at hand.

Seen through the eyes of a Classics teacher, there is one positive aspect of these reforms: the conservation of Ancient Civilisation as a compulsory subject for all students of the general upper secondary school. This will be taken in the second year with a total of 75 hours. From 1988 until now it has been taught in the last year of the *Gymnasium* with a slightly higher number of lessons. Consequently, the school year 2006/7 will be a very busy year for the Danish teachers of Ancient Civilisation since lessons will be doubled up, when both the final-year students of the old system and the second-year students of the new system all take Ancient Civilisation at one and the same time – and with different study programmes.

The nature of Classics in Denmark

Ancient Greek and Latin in general

In Denmark, the study of Ancient Greek and Latin in the upper secondary school at whatever level seeks to combine the linguistic approach of the subject with the cultural. Over time, more and more focus has been attributed to the interpretation and the cultural understanding of the texts read, but linguistic precision is still appreciated as the means through which the full understanding of a given text will evolve. The systematic approach to all levels of Ancient Greek and Latin make these subjects equal in quality with Mathematics and Physics. Recent analyses of students after their graduation from the *Gymnasium* show that the students with a Classical A-level background together with those leaving school with an A-level in Mathematics and Physics are the most likely candidates to pursue their university studies with greater depth and success.

Latin at all levels is taught with the scope of giving the students first hand knowledge of Latin both as the language of the Romans and as the international European language of communication in literature, science and religion throughout European history up until recent times. Equally, the students should also be shown the close bond between Ancient Greek and the Roman culture. The aim is to make the students able to understand their own cultural identity and realise their linguistic and cultural heritage in a more international context. The systematic study of Latin should strengthen their linguistic imagination and be supportive of their learning of any modern language.

Latin at optional C-level

The students will have some experience of Latin from the General Linguistics course taught in the first half-year of their upper secondary education. The teacher can therefore choose whether to have an introduction phase with adapted texts or not. In any case the class will have to read a series of original Latin texts from before 150 CE. At least three authors should be read. There is no fixed number of pages to be read. The students will have to learn only the morphology and syntax needed to read the texts in question, and they will focus on achieving a basic Latin vocabulary, a general knowledge of Roman history and an understanding of the role of Latin in relation to the later European languages.

The new C-level will have an oral examination in a new form. The students will (in groups of between one and four) be given an unknown text of about one page of Latin supplemented by a short introduction, a free Danish translation of the text itself and a translation of up to three pages more of the same work and/or author to set the text in a wider context. The groups will have 24 hours to prepare a precise translation of the text and the linguistic commentary as well as the interpretation and general presentation of the meaning of the text. Each student will be examined on a third of the text prepared. The examination embraces four disciplines: reading out loud (in Latin) using the revised pronunciation or *pronuntiatio restituta*, translation, commentary on morphology and syntax and textual interpretation. The examination is a dialogue between the student and the teacher. An external examiner from another school takes notes and suggests a mark after the examination. The teacher and external examiner must agree on the mark given.

A-level Latin

A-level Latin is a two and a half year subject following directly after the introductory first half-year where the students have already been introduced to Latin through the General Linguistics course. The students reading A-level Latin have chosen this as one of the two to three core subjects of their education.

The A-level students will mainly read philosophical, rhetorical, political and poetic texts from the period before 150 CE. The reading will be organised thematically. Some texts will be read only cursorily or in translation. There is no fixed number of pages to be read. Before the reform, A-level students would read about 100 pages of original Latin texts and about 150 pages in translation. The students are also to study Roman art and architecture as well as the main aspects of Roman history, society and culture. At least one of the themes to be read should concern the Latin tradition after antiquity. All themes read should be given a modern perspective, and possibilities of collaborative work with other subjects (Mathematics and Science, Geography, Social Science, Greek/Ancient Civilisation, modern languages, Danish, etc.) should be sought out.

At A-level a thorough knowledge of Latin morphology and syntax is demanded as well as a basic Latin vocabulary. The students should be well acquainted with the patterns of word formation in Latin as well as in Danish and be able to explain the impact of Latin on modern languages concerning word formation, especially in scientific language.

There is a written as well as an oral examination. The written examination is a centrally set assignment (from the Ministry of Education). The subject is not known beforehand. The assignment contains a Latin text of between one and one and a half pages, followed by a free modern translation. The students are to translate one passage more closely to the original Latin text, to answer questions on syntax, to interpret the meaning of the text and to answer a series of questions concerning background knowledge with relation to the assignment, including analyses of images and modern perspectives on the text. The duration of the examination is five hours. The marks are given by a panel of examiners (two examiners for each assignment). The teacher of the class is not involved in the evaluation of the written assignments.

The oral examination concerns the texts read in class. Each student will be examined on half a page of the thoroughly read Latin texts for a period of 30 minutes (with a previous preparation period also of 30 minutes). The examination embraces reading out loud (in Latin), translation, morphology and syntax with relation to the text and textual interpretation. The examination is a dialogue between the student and the teacher. An examiner from another school takes notes and suggests a mark after the examination. Teacher and examiner must agree on the mark given.

Ancient Greek

Ancient Greek as a subject in the Danish school system concerns Greek antiquity as the basis for European culture. Greek original texts and monuments are studied to give the students an impression of the values, ideas and artistic idioms that have been so influential on later European culture. The texts and material remains are to be studied in their own historical context as well as in perspective. This should make the students able to understand their own culture and to reflect on the similarities and differences between this and other cultures. The methodology of the study of Greek should enable the students to deal with many different questions and problems concerning language and humanities in general and thus qualify them for further studies in various fields.

C-level Ancient Greek is a one-year free optional subject. In the beginning of the year, the main stress should be laid on learning the basic grammar and vocabulary. Cultural aspects, however, should be considered concurrently even from the first phase. The texts to be read are easy or even adapted texts from the Classical or Hellenistic period. The students should only learn the grammar needed to read the texts in question. A basis vocabulary is to be learned. A general knowledge of languages should be obtained by discussing similarities and differences between Ancient Greek and Danish in connection with translating from one language to the other. Greek words and concepts in modern European languages should also be discussed.

The optional C-level Greek has an oral examination. This is based on the texts read in class only. Each student will be examined in about a third of a page of Greek text for 25 minutes (with a prior preparation period of 25 minutes). The examination embraces reading out loud (in Greek using the Erasmian pronunciation), translation, morphology and syntax with relation to the text and textual interpretation. The relevant later perspectives on the text should also be presented.

A-level Ancient Greek is a two and a half year core subject to be studied together with A-level Latin. Both subjects begin immediately after the introductory first half-year of the general upper secondary education. The linguistic level obtained through the General Linguistics course forms the starting point for both A-levels.

In A-level Ancient Greek, the texts to be read date from Homer to Aristotle. Homer and Plato are compulsory authors. At least five literary genres must be studied in depth. Among these, the epic, historic, philosophical and rhetorical genres are compulsory. The last genre is optional and can be chosen from lyric poetry, drama, biography or scientific texts. Part of the reading will be organised thematically. At least three major themes should be chosen. In the thematic reading, some texts will be thoroughly read, others will be read more rapidly, and others again in translation with occasional verification of the translation in the original Greek text. All parts of the subject (including art and archaeology) must be seen in a later European perspective. In the thematic reading, the point of departure may be either a modern issue to be followed backwards in time to the very roots or an original Greek issue to be studied in its development through time. Collaboration with other subjects on the perspectives of later periods is an obvious opportunity. Part of the thematic reading may be organised as more independent work supported by ICT. At least one project should be organised as an e-learning project.

The regulations for the examinations in Greek follow the same pattern as the examinations in Latin (see above).

Ancient Civilisation

Ancient Civilisation as a subject was invented in 1903 to compensate for the loss of Ancient Greek as a compulsory subject for all. The main focus has always been on the Greek roots of European culture. The students do not read *about* antiquity, but study both original texts (in Danish translation) and important monuments (architecture, sculpture and vase painting). With the new reform, knowledge of the Roman period also will be required. As a consequence of this, there will be less time attributed to the Greek part of the subject. Previously, Homer, Plato and Attic drama were compulsory. With the reform this is no longer possible. The subject is to be studied in five 'columns' of which one is centred on images and four on texts. In the column concerning history of art, the class will have to choose only one field, either architecture or sculpture or vase painting, while previously all three fields were required. As in A-level Ancient Greek, all parts of the subject (including the monuments) must be seen in a later European perspective.

Ancient Civilisation has an oral examination of 30 minutes with a previous preparation period of one hour. Each student is given a page and a half of Greek (or Latin) text in translation chosen from the basic texts read in class. For perspective each student is also given an unseen text of between two and five pages from a later European period or an image of a

Greek or Roman monument with up to three unseen images of relevant later monuments for comparison.

Cross-curricular activity

The key feature of the new reform is cross-curricular activity. For students who have chosen A-level Ancient Greek and A-level Latin there will be a high degree of collaboration between the two subjects, and in the third year the students will write a small thesis on a Classical subject. If the students have chosen other core subjects, the thesis will be written within these.

All subjects give a tenth of their total number of lessons to cross-curricular activity with the scope of preparing the students for further, more independent studies. In the cross-curricular projects to be constructed at least two of the following fields must be present:

* science
* social science
* humanities.

Teachers are required to do much more cross-curricular collaboration since the reform than before.

Classics in the modern world

The modern world is a high-speed global world where technology plays an increasing role for travel, commerce and exchange of information. The technological development has given man more possibilities and choices than ever before in history. But there are dangers in all this. If you take all the beautiful bright colours and mix them together, the beauty and variety disappears and it becomes all brown. Similarly in the global world, it is important for all countries and peoples not to lose their individuality, their language and their cultural roots.

For Western European civilisation, Classics remind us that there is a long history behind us, beginning with the Ancient Greeks and Romans. Classics make us realise our linguistic as well as normative and cultural roots. Becoming rootless is another danger of the modern world. The study of Classics helps us to realise our cultural heritage and background, and the meticulous methodical approach that is needed to learn and understand the ancient languages shows us that not everything can be learned and understood in a wink and a zap, but that real learning takes time, training and tears.

The new technology, however, forms a major resource in modern teaching of Classics. ICT-based teaching gives us possibilities that we would otherwise not possess. Distance learning, online learning and e-learning are all new aspects to be taken into account in Classics as well as other areas. A whole new didactic methodology must be developed to explore the possibilities at hand. In the Danish school system, the new reform demands much more focus on ICT in all subjects, including Classics. Classics are already very well represented on the Internet in many different languages. Danish students have the advantage of being quite good at English, which means that the many English-language ICT facilities are open to them as well as the resources extant in their native language.

Teacher training

Danish teachers of Ancient Greek or Latin have all studied these subjects at university. Classics can be read at three universities in Denmark: the University of Copenhagen, the University of Aarhus and the University of Southern Denmark in Odense. Classical Archaeology is separated from the philological studies and can be read only in Copenhagen and Aarhus. The study of Classical Archaeology does not qualify students to teach Classics in the general upper secondary school.

Danish upper secondary teachers are normally not required to teach subjects other than their university subjects. The university subjects can be very freely combined, so while some teachers may have Ancient Greek and Latin, others may have Latin and English, Ancient Greek and Danish, Latin and Mathematics or other combinations. The university study of Ancient Greek qualifies graduates to teach Ancient Civilisation, but for the last 30 years or so, Ancient Civilisation has also been a subject in its own right at university level (though not as a main subject). Earlier, many teachers with related subjects like History, Religion, Latin and Philosophy were given dispensation to teach Ancient Civilisation.

The university education is followed by a teacher training course which now lasts for two years. This course contains practical teaching periods and theoretical elements, as well as assignments. It also includes a course on the pedagogical use of ICT.

Epilogue

I have just talked to a colleague on the phone. He has taught Latin at all levels for many years. His second subject is French and he also teaches Ancient Civilisation on dispensation. He told me that he had just removed all his Latin school books and notes from his apartment and put them in boxes in the basement. His French books have gone the same way (French and other modern languages apart from English have also suffered badly in the new reform). He reckons that he is never going to teach A-C level Latin or French again. Being the only Latin teacher at his school, he will have to take care of the Latin part of General Linguistics for all the first-year classes (8 to 10 classes of about 28 students each) in their first half-year. What is left for him is thus a very busy autumn season with

General Linguistics for about 225 students plus normal teaching of a few classes in Ancient Civilisation. In the spring season there will be only the few classes in Ancient Civilisation left to teach. My colleague will never again be able to have a full-time job with a normal schedule. This is not an unusual situation and many teachers of Classics who do not have other subjects to fall back on are in a similar position. This is sad, and the more so because teaching Classics is not just a job you do to earn a living – it is a way of life, a way of thinking, a special way of being. But we should not give up. I cling to the words of Herodotus about big cities becoming small and *vice versa*. Classics can never die.

France

Odile Denis-Laroque (with John Bulwer)

The basic organisation of language teaching in France means that the function of the Classics teacher differs slightly from that of some other countries. The nearest equivalent is *professeur de lettres classiques* (teacher of Classical literature). This, however, indicates that the teacher is not only qualified to teach both Latin and Greek, but is also one of the team in the school who take the French language (mother tongue) classes. An important part of their work, therefore, is concerned with French language and literature, as well as with the ancient languages. Others in the team teaching French will be *professeurs de lettres modernes* (teachers of modern literature), who have a different training and who are not qualified to teach Latin or Greek but who may have studied Latin at university, or at least another modern language. The level of qualification in French is the same, but the Classics teacher has to achieve a high level in Latin and Greek as well. Both branches study the same six authors in French, but the Classicists go on to study four Latin and four Greek authors, while the modernists do comparative literature and then Latin or a modern language, as well as linguistics and early French.

In some institutions there is still quite a lot of Latin for the students of *lettres modernes*: an obligatory course either in literature and civilisation (with texts in translation) or in language at an appropriate level including beginners. In addition a Latin translation paper is optional for the competitive examination for the secondary level teaching qualification *CAPES (Certificat d'Aptitude au Professorat de l'Enseignement Secondaire)* and obligatory at the higher level teaching qualification *Agrégation*. Once qualified, the teachers go on to obtain posts in schools, which are classified as *lettres classiques* or *lettres modernes*, although they both cover the teaching of French. There are many more posts for *professeurs de lettres modernes* than for their Classical colleagues. It would be most unusual if a *professeur de lettres classiques* were to teach only Latin and Greek. They always take some French classes. Nonetheless, of the 3,000 teachers appointed through the competition for newly qualified teachers in 2002 (*CAPES*) to teach French in schools, nearly 600 were appointed as *professeurs de lettres classiques*.

Although these teachers would normally have studied both Latin and Greek at school, it is now possible for them to begin Latin and Greek at university provided that they reach the required level by the end of their studies. The breadth of the final *Baccalauréat* programme means that some decisions can be postponed and even a mainly scientific set of options can be converted later to a literary study at university.

Latin and Greek have always had a place in the national curriculum, although this place has undergone a number of recent reforms. These changes are generally seen as attacks on the status of the subject and have provoked considerable reaction. Up to 1968 only the best performing pupils were allowed to take Latin after a period of observation. They continued with a generous timetable allocation. After 1968 the languages became optional and were open to pupils of all abilities. Secondary education in France is divided between the *collège* and the *lycée*. The *collège* takes pupils between 11 and 14, and the *lycée* takes the pupils of the final three years, from 15 to 18. In the *collège* pupils can begin Latin at the age of 12 and can continue for two years. Greek is introduced later but can be studied alongside Latin, although with a reduced timetable. Greek is often squeezed in in this way owing to the demands of other subjects on the timetable. When the pupils move to the *lycée* Latin can be continued as an optional subject. There are three possible ways in which this can be done and this alters the way in which it is assessed in the final examinations. All take the *Baccalauréat* in one of three branches: in Arts and Human Sciences (L), in Science (S) or in Social and Economic Sciences (ES). All take Philosophy as a compulsory subject in the final year. In all official documents classes are referred to by their number. As the year number goes down, the older the pupil becomes. There are seven years of secondary education. Thus 6th class refers to pupils aged 11, 5th to 12-year-olds, and so on until 1st class which is the penultimate year of school (16 years); the final year is called *terminale*.

The subject is always timetabled as Latin or Greek. There are no courses in Classical Civilisation, although the content of the language courses has changed in recent years to incorporate much more non-linguistic material. However, high emphasis is placed on language learning, and grammatical knowledge is valued. The close connection between French language teaching and Latin is a sign of the general objective of the Classics teacher: it is for language learning. Although reading the Latin historians would be part of the course, History itself tends to be regarded as a separate subject. Ancient History and Latin or Greek, while related, are not as closely linked as they may be in other countries. The content of lessons has evolved recently and more emphasis is placed on the context of the target language. This is seen often in an emphasis on authentic texts in the course books, even in the earliest chapters. The objective of their study is that the pupils should be able to read and understand a text of a suitable level of difficulty, and then be able to translate it. Language features studied may vary according to the texts but they should acquire by the end of their time in the *collège* a vocabulary of between 800 and 1,000 words which are chosen for their relevance to French. The reading aloud of texts studied is seen as an important support to the objective of reading and understanding of the texts studied. At the *lycée* the language learning has the added objective of contributing to the development of individual thinking and to a sense of citizenship.

The learning aim is to read authentic texts as accurately as possible. The emphasis is always on authenticity from the beginning and little use is made of extensive synthetic Latin. The approach is close reading rather than rapid reading, and always with an emphasis on the close connection to French. The *approfondissement* or in-depth analysis of the pupils' first language is the major justification for the learning of Latin. In contrast Greek is regarded as interesting in itself. In addition, it is important to the development of specialists in literature and social sciences, and in contributing to an awareness of the linguistic and cultural heritage of the Classical world. The move to the use of authentic original texts is completed at the *lycée*. Teachers tend to find that the younger pupils respond well to the demands made on them owing to their natural curiosity and enthusiasm. Older pupils who have opted for the subject show their aptitude and competence for the languages. However, the intermediate classes can pose problems for the teacher who may have to deal with those who have opted to continue alongside those who have not and may consequently lose interest. From good numbers beginning Latin, the number of those continuing is much lower, particularly at university level. Certain institutions do very well to keep their pupils through to the end of their studies.

In view of the progress made in the development of new teaching methods, it is recognised that there is a difference of attitude between more traditional teachers and more progressive ones. The reforms after 1968 indicate this. A more traditional approach involves an emphasis on language learning and grammatical knowledge, and assumes that an ability to take Latin is a mark of the more intelligent pupil. A more progressive approach would offer Latin and Greek to all levels of ability and would encourage a wider range of non-linguistic elements to the Latin lessons. However, the change of attitude can also be seen in the way that teachers of Latin and Greek argue for their subject. No longer is it seen as a mark of the best pupil to take Latin and Greek, preparing for entry to further study at university at the highest level. It is seen more as a cultural complement: the foundation of European culture and society. Thus it is a subject which is relevant to all in French society, to lose which would be to cut the current generation off from its cultural roots. Classics is seen as a subject which can contribute towards a general education for the pupil, as opposed to a purely scientific or technical one. The breadth and pluralism of the *Baccalauréat* is regarded as important: a pupil should emerge from school as a well-rounded individual, a good citizen with a grounding in both arts and sciences. In a recent crisis where a reform has been announced to group classes in large city *lycées* to make them more economically viable, the publicity raised in protest has concentrated on this angle. The distinguished Classicist Jacqueline de Romilly wrote an appeal in the *Figaro* which emphasises the cultural legacy of Classical studies:

On oublie trop facilement semble-t-il que l'enseignement est aussi une formation de l'esprit, une formation du caractère, du jugement, de l'imagination – et une découverte des valeurs. Or, tout cela a commencé dans les civilisations antiques. (We forget too easily, it seems, that education is also a formation of the mind, a formation of the personality, of judgement, of the imagination – and a discovery of values. Now all this has its origin in the ancient civilisations.)

In addition the closeness of the two languages to French is regarded as culturally important:

Pour m'en tenir aux deux options que sont le latin et le grec, il est clair que ces deux disciplines étaient, dès le principe, étroitement liées au français. Elles représentent le point de départ de notre langue et de notre culture; ce sont nos racines. Ces deux langues étudiées assez tôt, développent la compréhension de nos mots et de nos constructions; or, l'on sait assez les difficultés que connaît aujourd'hui le français ... (To keep to the two options of Latin and Greek, it is clear that these two disciplines from the outset are closely linked to French. They represent the point of departure of our language and culture; they are our roots. These two languages, studied at an early age, develop a comprehension of our vocabulary and our constructions; and we know well enough the difficulties that French has these days ...)

Finally she evokes an image which compares Latin and Greek to threatened natural species which deserve a special protected status:

D'ailleurs, n'existe-t-il pas, pour la faune et pour la flore des espèces protégées, quand des menaces extérieures tendent à trop réduire leur nombre? (Besides doesn't this [protected status] exist for protected species of plants and animals, when external forces threaten to reduce their numbers too much?)

An article by Bertrand Poirot-Delpech in *Le Monde*, also arguing against the recent proposed reforms, makes the point that numbers may actually have gone up in recent years:

... mais le nombre des élèves en langues anciennes est plus élevé, en chiffre absolu, qu'au temps glorieux des sections A. Mais en quoi les filières du secondaire seraient-elles moins 'élitistes' si on y supprime un peu partout les options de latin et de grec? (... but the number of pupils of ancient languages, in absolute terms, is higher than in the glory days of the A section of the Baccalaureate. How will the different branches of the secondary school be less elitist if the Latin and Greek options are closed almost everywhere?)

The sources for these quotations can be found on the CNARELA website (http://www.cnarela.asso.fr).

This change of attitude has been accompanied by a modernisation of teaching methods. Given that the teachers of Latin and Greek also teach French, the development of methods in French pedagogy has had a parallel effect in Latin and Greek.

It would be surprising if a change of style in one subject area were not accompanied by a similar change in others. This joint responsibility for French and for Classics has led to a considerable change in attitude on the part of Classics teachers. New types of material were developed first in the local associations of teachers, which are coordinated by CNARELA (*Coordination Nationale des Associations Régionales des Enseignants de Langues Anciennes*, National Coordination of the Regional Associations of Teachers of Ancient Languages). The regional associations are based in nearly all major French cities and come to about 30 in number, including a travel agency devoted to school trips to areas of interest to those pupils studying Classical subjects (Thalassa). The website for CNARELA contains details of many documents and publications developed originally in the regional associations to be of direct assistance to teachers in their work (http://www.cnarela.asso.fr). These range from pedagogical theory to practical interpretation of texts and themes; topics cover all aspects of the Classical world from religion, mythology, history and society to language and literature. The local associations also organise *journées des langues anciennes* in their local areas, where for a number of days activities involving Classical subjects are held, which may range from talks and visits to dramatic performances and films. These form part of the campaigns to promote Classics in schools.

Undoubtedly teachers of Latin and Greek feel that they are under pressure from government reforms. They feel that as the state system has employed them to do a particular job, they deserve rather more support than they get from the government. Even teachers who incline to the more traditional ways of thinking are still appointed members of the state system and feel as though they should be used accordingly. They feel that the representatives of the state make public announcements that are broadly in favour of learning Classical subjects, but that their actions lead directly to a deterioration of the situation. They regard the government position as at best ambiguous.

The above remarks all apply to state schools, operating under the national system of education for the whole of France. In contrast to many other countries Latin and Greek maintain a strong presence in the national system. There are private schools which for the most part have a religious foundation. The teaching of Latin and Greek in these schools (particularly Latin) may well reflect the concerns of the Church with the official language of the Vatican. Teaching may also be undertaken by those in religious orders. Most of the innovations have taken place within the state system (which is secular) and have then found their way into the private sector. The close connection between the private schools and the Church gives an image of Classics in these schools a rather ecclesiastical overtone, in contrast to the secular and more radical image encouraged in the state schools.

Germany

Hans-Joachim Glücklich

The federal structure of Germany

Germany is a federal republic of 16 states. According to the constitution of the Federal Republic of Germany the states are responsible for cultural affairs and for education. Therefore, every state has a ministry (department) for Education and Cultural Affairs or two separate ministries. Also there is a federal minister of Cultural Affairs who tries to coordinate the state activities and to support certain developments, including financial ones such as the development of full-time schools. Every state not only has individual vacation times – in order to avoid motorway traffic problems – but also individual regulations for the number of years spent in school (12 or 13). It is also responsible for school types and the curriculum.

Addresses of the departments for culture and education of the German states can be found at www.bildungsserver.de/zeigen.html?seite=580

The German school system

The so-called linked school system consists of primary and secondary education. Primary education comprises the 1st to 4th grades; secondary education comprises the 5th to 12th or 13th grades and is divided into level I (5th to 10th grades) and level II (11th to 12th or 13th grades). The 5th and 6th grades are called the orientation or guidance level (*Orientierungsstufe*); in some states they are joined to the primary education, in other states to the secondary education. The secondary education and the grades are not part of one type of school. There are different school types and consequently different transitions and examinations or graduations.

Types of secondary school

There are a number of types of secondary schools. The *Hauptschule* is for those pupils who do not want to go to any other school type or do not qualify for one. The *Realschule* is for those pupils who do not intend to take the Baccalaureate and so qualify for studies at university. The *Gymnasium* is for those who mostly want to pass the Baccalaureate and gain entrance to a university. Comprehensive schools (*Gesamtschulen*) may unite all types of school either just because they are on the same site or in the same building (*kooperative Gesamtschule*) or because they have a management that continually checks if pupils qualify to switch from one type to another (*integrierte Gesamtschule*). A *Gymnasium* can be focused on languages, on science or on music or have several focuses. Classical *Gymnasiums* (*Altsprachliche Gymnasien*) demand the learning of three languages, Latin, English and Greek or French. But it is possible to learn more languages on a voluntary basis. For those who choose Greek in the 8th grade, a voluntary course in French is offered in the 11th grade. Greek is taught mostly in the Classical *Gymnasium*, where a third foreign language (either Greek or French) is obligatory, but it can also be taught in other types of school as an optional subject.

1-4	elementary school	*Primarstufe*	*Grundschule*		
			school type recommended by teachers of elementary school		
5-6	orientation level	*Orientierungs-stufe*	*Hauptschule*	*Realschule*	*Gymnasium*
					school type recommended by teachers of the gymnasium
7-9			*Hauptschule*		
7-10	high school	*Sekundarstufe I*	*Hauptschule*	*Realschule*	*Gymnasium*
			qualified *Hauptschul-abschluss*	*Realschul-abschluss*	*Realschul-abschluss*
11-12 or 11-13	college	*Sekundarstufe II*			*Gymnasium*
					Abitur
			kooperative Gesamtschule (different types of school in one institution)	*kooperative Gesamtschule*	*kooperative Gesamtschule*
			integrierte Gesamtschule (different types of school in one school with the continuous possibility of changing to another type of school according to the qualification)		

Differences in the school systems of the states

The system described above shows a lot of variation among the different states. The elementary school usually consists of four years, but in some states it is six. The change to another school type consequently takes place either after the 4th or after the 6th grade. In those states where the transition from one type to another takes place after the 6th grade, sometimes pupils who choose Latin as a language for the 5th grade are allowed to switch after the 4th grade to a so-called *Altsprachliches Gymnasium* (*Gymnasium* with focus on Classical languages). In addition the number of cooperative or integrated comprehensive schools varies significantly from state to state according to the political orientation (socialist/green, conservative/liberal) of the government.

More and more states are reducing the number of years in secondary education so that everyone is in school from the 5th to the 12th grade. After the reunification of Germany in 1990 there was a difference between the Eastern German states, who finished secondary education after the 12th grade, and the Western German states, who finished after the 13th grade. In a long period of transition some Eastern German states switched to 13 years of primary and secondary education, some Western German states to 12 years. Now most states will introduce the 12-year-long primary and secondary education with the final examination (graduation from secondary school, known as the *Abitur* and equivalent to the Baccalaureate) after 12 years. This will make the German school system more comparable with the system in other countries. Because of the new length of college level II, new curricula are being planned or have been written already.

In most states the transition to secondary education can be made after the 4th grade, in some after the 6th grade. The 5th and 6th grades are called orientation level (*Orientierungsstufe*). If this orientation level is integral in a high school, it is nevertheless possible to switch to another school type after the 6th grade. This depends on the advice of school class conferences. The class conference is a formal meeting of each pupil's teachers, chaired by a member of the management team, which at the end of each school year discusses the pupil's progress and has the power to pass the pupil to the following year, or to require that he or she repeat the year. This is a common practice in many European countries. In this case the class conference must agree to a change of school. If the orientation level is integral in an elementary school, the pupils who qualify can switch to a high school. Those who decide to learn Latin starting at the 5th grade start in orientation levels that are joined to a *Gymnasium*.

Curricula of the states of the Federal Republic of Germany

The curriculum of each state can be found either via
www.bildungsserver.de/drucken.html?seite=400 or directly at
http://db.kmk.org/lehrplan/

This curriculum data bank makes it possible to find the curricula of all states and subjects and authorities or publishers for ordering them.

School laws can be found at www.bildungsserver.de/zeigen.html?seite=72

The names and addresses of all the German state departments for education can be found at www.bildungsserver.de/zeigen.html?seite=580

A map of the German states can be found at www.Deutscher Bildungsserver.de – Lehrplan-Datenbank. There the individual states can be clicked on, and then the curricula found. These curricula mostly start by giving reasons for learning Latin and Greek, then list the subjects and abilities that are to be achieved, show what standards of knowledge and ability must be attained, and state in what year they must be introduced. However, mostly they leave some freedom in the sequences of learning because the sequence of subjects depends on the textbook introduced in the individual school. In Germany many different elementary textbooks are permitted for use in schools.

Standards of education

By the end of the 10th grade certain standards have to be fulfilled in order for the pupil to be allowed to change to the secondary level II. Until 2004 these standards were described in some curricula and were fulfilled if the student reached the end of the 10th grade successfully. Now some states have started to give detailed lists of these standards and even plan a kind of examination. This development is caused by the political intention first to set equal standards across all states of the Federal Republic of Germany, and later to have standards that equate to those of other European countries.

Subjects and objectives

In the German higher education system Latin and Greek belong to the so-called linguistic-literary-artistic field. Generally the reasons for learning Latin are given as follows:

- The students understand their own native language and linguistic structures better by contrast with Latin.
- Their ability to express thoughts in an appropriate way is improved because they learn new thoughts and facts together with new Latin words and have to find the appropriate German expression.
- Latin provides the knowledge of important bases of European culture and history, forms an awareness of European history, and develops a European identity.
- Latin trains reading competence, the ability to reflect on language and texts and to interpret texts in an appropriate and reliable way.
- Latin helps to acquire fundamental knowledge of grammar and semantics that makes it easier to learn other languages.

61

- Dealing with the contents of Latin texts and with their literary and linguistic form leads to a way of thinking that is analytic and connected with other fields; it enables pupils to connect different fields and subjects, the past and the present, and this means they will be able to transfer knowledge to another field and to think scientifically or in a scholarly way.
- The basic works of Classical authors and writers of a later time, including Christian authors, should be read, because Latin was the *lingua franca* for 2,000 years and because Latin texts transformed and developed Greek thoughts, show their own values and beauty, mixed ancient and Christian thoughts and formed the European mind.
- Dealing with important fundamental questions of human life like love, state, government, society, law and justice, philosophy and religion leads pupils to adopt a position towards values and helps them to find a responsible way to live their lives.
- Dealing with the tradition and reception of Latin texts develops consciousness of European fundamentals and is helpful for an aesthetic education.

The reasons for learning Greek are presented in a similar way to those for learning Latin. In addition the following reasons are given:

- Dealing with Greek myths shows different ways of thinking and helps the pupil to understand European art and literature that have been influenced and still are influenced by Greek myths.
- Dealing with Greek art, and dealing with fundamental European thoughts and works of literature allows the pupil to come across them in their original and authentic statement.
- The chance to compare Ancient Greek with Modern Greek allows an easy transfer.

It is not intended to discuss, to explain or to question these reasons here, but at least it should be added that Latin and Greek language and works of literature are themselves of great, sometimes unrivalled, and singular beauty. And finally too films are accepted as an important part of the tradition of Roman and Greek literature.

Graduation from the *Gymnasium* (*Abitur*)

More and more states use a central examination: all students have to take this examination on the same day. Some states still have an individual written examination, and in this case the teacher of every 12th or 13th class has to send two different suggestions for the written examination to the Ministry of Education; on the day of the written examination a sealed envelope is opened and one of the suggestions will be indicated to have been chosen for the examination.

The new coordinated standards for the final examination (*Einheitliche*

Prüfungsanforderungen in der Abiturprüfung, EPA) can be downloaded as PdF-files from the internet. The standards describe objectives, methods and criteria for marks in Latin and Greek examinations and give examples.

Start and length of courses in Latin and Greek

Latin

In Germany Latin can be learned starting in the 5th grade, in the 7th grade, in the 9th grade and in the 11th grade. Accordingly the course types are called Latin I, Latin II, Latin III and Latin IV. There are also Latin courses at the universities for those students who did not learn Latin in school but need to show knowledge of Latin for certain fields and graduations. Every university has its own regulations as to which fields require this so-called *Latinum*. The learners have to pass a written examination and an oral examination that must be taken in front of a board of examiners in order to coordinate the requirements and to assure equal conditions.

As the different ways of beginning Latin show, there are different languages to begin with in school and different sequences of languages such as English–Latin–French or English–French–Latin. But, in addition, those who start Latin in the 5th grade have already started English in the 3rd or 4th grade. Therefore, the Classical *Gymnasium* (*Altsprachliches Gymnasium*) offers two or three English lessons per week in addition to the five Latin lessons in the 5th grade in order to maintain and develop the knowledge of English already acquired. This can be seen in the innovative *Biberacher Modell* (www.navonline.de/aktuell/ausbildung/akt_ausbildung_lateinplus.php) and the *Latein plus-project* of Rhineland-Palatinate at http://latein-plus.bildung-rp.de/

The Latin courses I, II, III and IV all have as their aims the acquisition of knowledge of Latin grammar, and of the ability to understand Latin texts and to give a basic interpretation based on semantics, grammar and style. The methods of the courses are somewhat different at the levels of both grammar and literature. The longer the courses are, the more induction in grammar is possible and the more translation skills can be acquired. The short courses reduce the grammar to basic knowledge, use deduction and comparison with other languages, and reduce the amount of texts and interpretation.

Greek

Greek lessons start in the 8th grade of the Classical *Gymnasium* (*Altsprachliches Gymnasium*), but other types of schools sometimes offer Greek on a voluntary basis.

Latin and Greek in the secondary level II

In the secondary level II languages can be studied as a main or full course (*Leistungskurs*) with five lessons per week or in a shorter basic course (*Grundkurs*) with three lessons a week. Full courses offer a large programme of literature and train skills like interpretation, discussion, talks, writing and presenting papers, use of grammar books, dictionaries, bibliographies and websites. The written examination is required only for full courses.

Latinum and *Graecum*

Knowledge of Latin or the so-called *Latinum* certificate is required for certain fields, often for entrance to a doctorate. But universities show discrepancies in their requirements, which are sometimes difficult to understand. Personal research at the university or institute is recommended. From time to time the ministries of Culture and the German Association of Teachers of Latin and Greek, *Deutscher Altphilologenverband* (DAV), in its periodical *Forum Classicum* (see below) publish surveys of the requirements at each university based on recent research at the universities. The *Latinum* will be given

(a) after a certain number of years of Latin (in Latin I and II five years, in other types three to four years),
(b) if the mark at the end of the lessons is not lower than 4 (D), and
(c) if the ability to translate easy texts of Caesar and Cicero (speeches) can be proved by the results of classroom tests.

Knowledge of Greek or the proof of a so-called *Graecum* is required for the study of Latin, Ancient History, Classical Archaeology and Philosophy.

Number of students at school

Latin enjoys the favour of parents and pupils to some extent. About 679,000 students learn Latin at schools in Germany every year (about 28% of students in higher secondary education). In the western part of Germany it could be claimed that the schools that offer Latin in the 5th grade have almost become popular, as the annual number of new pupils can prove. They offer English in addition to Latin because pupils started with English in the 3rd or 4th grade and are not supposed to forget it; but they do not make English in the 5th grade relevant for marks and tests. The chances of comparing Latin and Greek and of combining the methods of speaking and of observing languages are considered to be excellent for education. At present Latin is the third most learned language in schools, with English in first place and French in second. The course types Latin I and II are either consolidated or growing; the type Latin III is losing some pupils. In the 11th and 12th grades after years of losses there seems to be a stabilised or slowly increasing number of students.

Greek is studied by about 13,500 students in schools every year.

Principles of teaching

Curricula and teachers mostly separate Latin studies into two parts: a grammar and a literature phase. But there are tendencies to combine both steps, teaching grammar from texts without using them just as grammar material, and reading texts by applying text grammar and semantics.

In the literature study there is so-called work reading and author reading and subject-focused reading. In general all aspects are combined because excerpts of one work are read following a subject-focused interest (e.g. Caesar's *Bellum Gallicum* is read with a focus on 'politics and propaganda' or on the question of the *'bellum iustum'* or on the 'profile of a ruler'). Text extracts are carefully combined to form sequences with different focuses resulting in a good knowledge either of the different aspects of a work of literature or of a subject. Texts of Classical times are in the focal point, but modern texts are compared, as well as Latin texts of late antiquity, medieval times and the Renaissance. Medieval texts are often read directly after the elementary books because some of them have an almost German word order and therefore are easy to read. More and more learning and teaching methods are developed that reduce frontal and teacher-centred teaching. The so-called action-centred teaching tries to develop and to maintain the independence, activity and creativity of the pupils. Finally visits to museums, excursions, production of texts, participation in competitions, and projects that bring together several fields of school education are considered to play an important role in school.

Latin elementary books and text editions

Elementary books

All modern elementary books try to present texts and to teach grammar with texts. But most of them still fall back into some old-fashioned methods and explanations which only suit the translation into German, not the understanding of Latin, and often lead to a strange 'translation language' (*Übersetzungsdeutsch*) that is not a modern and real German. In this respect they are counter-productive to the aim of teaching German grammar and expressions through Latin. However, all modern elementary books succeed in presenting a comprehensive picture of ancient Rome and the Roman Empire because they present numerous pictures, provide a large amount of historic, archaeological and political information, and demonstrate the presence of Latin language and Roman culture and ideas in our time. They are very creative in presenting interesting and amusing exercises and in suggesting independent work by pupils.

The most popular books for Latin II, starting in the 7th grade, are: *Arcus* (1995), *Cursus continuus* (1995), *Felix* (1995), *Interesse* (1996), *Iter Romanum* (1996), *Lumina* (1998), *Ostia altera* (1995), *Prima* (2004) and *Salvete* (1995).

Text editions

Text editions offer text sequences with a synoptic vocabulary and historical and stylistic commentary; they give an explanation of the biography of the author, the social and historical circumstances, the reception and tradition of the text and modern aspects of its understanding. Therefore, they offer texts to promote an understanding of the historical background and reception texts that can be used for comparison. They also present tasks and suggestions as to how to work with the texts and interpret them. These tasks and propositions start with the observation of the text and its semantic, grammatical and stylistic features, continue with comparisons and finish with suggestions as to how to evaluate and enjoy the text or to make the thoughts of the text alive or working. The activity and the independence of pupils and students in working out an interpretation is encouraged and supported by new methods of activity-orientated tasks.

German publishers issue several series of books for classroom use which cover a number of authors and themes. The most important text editions of this kind are: *Altsprachliche Textausgaben* (published by Klett, since 1977); *Antike und Gegenwart* (published by Buchner, since 1990); and *Exempla* (published by Vandenhoeck and Ruprecht, since 1980).

There are also new editions for the transition to authentic texts and the first authentic texts that help with articulated presentation of the text (e.g. in colometric writing, see Appendix) and with repetitions or exercises of grammar. The course books named above have some additional volumes for early reading. They are: *Clara* (published by Vandenhoeck and Ruprecht, since 2002), *Transit* (published by Buchner, since 1994), and *Transfer* (published by Buchner, since 2003).

Greek elementary books and text editions

Elementary books

Greek is taught on the basis of texts. There are three recent Greek elementary books: *Hellas* (1999), *Lexis* (new edition 1988), and *Kantharos* (1982) with supplement *Kantharidion* (1997). The most used book seems to be *Kantharos*, which has longer texts than *Lexis*, but a shorter grammar course than *Hellas*. There are attempts to combine the learning of Ancient Greek with the learning of Modern Greek.

Text editions

Printing text editions for Greek classes is very expensive. It is very seldom that a modern text edition for schools is published. Teachers have to rely on older text editions, their own text arrangements and commentaries or copies of old editions. To date there is no data bank of texts for use in schools that could be downloaded from the web.

History of Classics teaching in Germany

Latin has been the main subject in higher education over centuries (Paulsen 1921). Latin has managed to survive all its critics and hostile attacks (see above in the section on numbers of pupils), even the attempt of 1968 to remove it from schools when S.R. Robinsohn wrote that Latin had no right to be a part of a modern curriculum (Robinsohn 1972). The German association of teachers of Latin and Greek (*Deutscher Altphilologenverband*, DAV) has found ways to refute this opinion and to publish good reasons for Latin being a part of the curriculum. Many of those reasons can be found and explained in Nickel (1978); Glücklich (1993); Maier (1979, 1984, 1985); and Westphalen (1992).

See also the publication 'Latinum. *Latein in der Schule und für das Studium*', edited by the DAV Commission for the *Latinum* (no year, at www.altphilologenverband.de). Today there is a secure position for Latin. Greek in the twentieth century has been mostly only a subject in Classical *Gymnasiums*. Now about 13,500 students choose Greek every year.

Didactics, methodology, bibliographies

Specific bibliographies are Müller and Schauer (1994) for Latin and Müller and Schauer (1996) for Greek. The above-mentioned works on didactics and methods of teaching Latin are still current (Nickel 1978; Glücklich 1993; Maier 1979, 1984, 1985; and Westphalen 1992). Of course there are new articles and some new books, but there is no new comprehensive book on teaching Latin and many articles in periodicals repeat what is written in the books above.

Periodicals for teaching Classics are *Der altsprachliche Unterricht* (Klett), *Forum Classicum* (DAV), the online periodical *Pegasus* (www.pegasus-onlinezeitschrift.de) and the newsletters of the state branches of DAV (see below). Also the periodical *Gymnasium* sometimes prints articles for teachers; it is useful because of its bibliographical surveys, its reviews and its articles on ancient literature and archaeology.

Teachers

There are between 9,000 and 10,000 teachers of Latin or Greek in Germany. Teachers of Greek generally teach Latin as well. Teachers of

Latin often teach also German, English, French, History, or Religion, and sometimes Music, Mathematics, or Biology. Most combinations are possible and allowed. Owing to many warnings from ministries the number of student teachers decreased steadily from 1990 to 2000. Now there is a shortage of teachers and the ministries encourage young students to study Latin. At present everyone who passes the second teacher's examination can hope to find employment. Those who study Ancient Greek are well advised to study not only Latin but a third additional subject as well; this will also make them employable in those schools that do not offer Greek. But at present even for teachers of Greek the chances of finding employment are very good because the average age of teachers of Greek is high and many of them will retire within the next few years.

Teachers in Germany are still mostly public servants with a good salary commensurate with the rate for high-level public servants. Young full-time teachers have to teach 25 or more lessons per week. Sometimes they have to give more than 25 lessons per week because there is a shortage of teachers at present and because they have to accrue time that they will get back as a reduction from 25 lessons when they are older.

The German Association of Teachers of Latin and Greek is called the *Deutscher Altphilologenverband* (DAV), while professors and teachers of Latin, Greek, Archaeology and Ancient History in universities have as their association the Mommsen Society (*Mommsen-Gesellschaft*). In 2005 the DAV had 6,000 members from a possible 9,000 or 10,000. The DAV holds a congress every two years with about 900 or more participants. At this congress the so-called Humanism Award is given to an outstanding personality who favours or can favour Classical education and humanism. It has most recently been awarded to Richard von Weizsäcker, Roman Herzog, Alfred Grosser and Wladislaw Bartoszewski.

The DAV website is www.altphilologenverband.de. The periodical of the DAV, *Forum Classicum*, can be described as the leading forum for discussions about aims, didactics and methods of teaching Latin and Greek. Its website is www.forum-classicum.de. There is also an interesting online periodical, *Pegasus* (www.pegasus-onlinezeitschrift.de). Moreover the DAV publishes, among other things, the periodical *Gymnasium*. Every state in Germany has its own branch of the DAV, and most of them have their own website and periodical. See for example the website of the Berlin and Brandenburg section: www.peirene.de.

Latin and Greek at university and teacher training

Studying Latin at university requires the *Latinum*, the proof of good knowledge of Latin. It also requires some knowledge of Ancient Greek. Students have to study two subjects at least, in some states three, in order to pass the final examination (*Erstes Staatsexamen*). The regulations of every university list the obligatory subjects in Latin: language, literature, translation from Latin, translation into Latin, knowledge of ancient authors and works and sometimes of medieval authors and works as well. In addition: linguistics, history of the Latin language, archaeology, ancient history, philosophy, pedagogy. At present most states want to increase the amount of pedagogy in the study, independent from Latin or Greek. This will result in a lack of broad knowledge of Latin literature and consequently also of Latin language and style. But it is a result of the tendencies to change the profile of teachers. Some ministries do not ask for the scholarly trained teacher who can show how to work and to read and to interpret from his own experience and who derives educational values from his subject. Instead they ask for the teacher who knows a lot about education and learning and social psychology as well as having a knowledge of Latin or Greek.

After the examination in university (*Erstes Staatsexamen*) students have to pass two years of teacher training (*Referendariat*), which ends with another examination (*Zweites Staatsexamen*) consisting of a demonstration of classroom competence, knowledge about didactics and methods and a written report about teaching. The length of this period of teacher training may be reduced in the future because didactics and pedagogy will be more integrated into the university studies and because there will be a shortage of teachers and they are needed fast.

All teachers have the right and the obligation to continue their studies of methods and to improve their knowledge in short courses. There is a large number of in-service training courses in every state.

Italy

Annarella Perra

Introduction

In Italy there is a long tradition of teaching Classics and for centuries it has been considered very important, not only because the Italian language is a Neo-Latin (or Romance) language, but also because *in primis* Latin studies represented and continue to represent today a fundamental linguistic base for the students to learn the lexicon, grammar and syntax of their mother tongue (Italian). In addition Ancient Greek has been studied together with Latin for many years in our country in the *Liceo Classico* (classical lyceum) for its cultural and educational value and its influence in the Western world before the predominance of Rome.

Teaching Classics in Italy: from its origins to the twenty-first century

In Italy Classics teaching has been greatly modified over the years by different reforms that have created a complex organisation in the Italian educational panorama. For many centuries Latin was the most important subject for training scholars in the humanistic period and it continued to hold on to this supremacy for a very long time. It was defined in an official way in the sixteenth and seventeenth centuries through the *Ratio Studiorum* (*Grammatica, Rhetorica, Latinitas Classicorum*), in the *Seminaria Nobilium* (Jesuit Colleges) in which Cicero (through his work *de officiis*) represented the only author worthy of being studied as a model. Ancient Greek initially was not included in the *Ratio Studiorum*. In 1859 the Casati Law introduced Ancient Greek for the first time with the creation of the *Liceo Classico*, governed then by the various regulations and programmes of 1860-2, in which about ten hours weekly were dedicated to teaching of this subject. In 1867 different introductory language instruction manuals were published for Ancient Greek (e.g. Curtius, Burnouf). At first Ancient Greek was taught only in the universities of Padua and Pavia.

Institutional programmes were written for the first time in 1893 (the *Martini Decretum*) and Greek became an optional subject for the first time in 1904 for the third year (last year of curriculum) of the *Liceo Classico*. Direct reading of Ancient Greek texts (Homer and tragedy or comedy) was introduced in 1911 by Minister Credaro. In this way Ancient Greek became an autonomous subject in the Italian upper secondary school from this period, but since 1923 until today only four hours a week are dedicated to this subject in the *Liceo Classico*. There have not really been great changes in the last hundred years, only some reduction and redefinition of programmes (the most important have been in 1965, 1967 and 1991).

Latin instead has undergone many redefinitions of its place in the school curriculum and has been modified widely. In 1923 Minister Gentile introduced Latin also to the second and third years of the secondary school for the first three years (*Scuola Media inferiore*, from 11 to 13 years of age in Italy), but in 1962 it became an optional subject in the third year and obligatory only in the second year. It ceased to be an obligatory subject for the first time at this school level in 1977. From that time until today Latin has been taught only in the Italian upper secondary school (*Scuola Media superiore*), from 14 to 18 years of age. In addition the number of hours dedicated to Latin has been greatly reduced: in 1860 there were 37 hours weekly, in 1880 32 hours and from 1923 until today generally five hours (except on experimental courses, such as the Brocca courses, see below).

All these reforms have not in any way modified the official programmes of the subjects nor their contents: teachers over the years have developed different methodologies and pedagogical approaches to the teaching of Latin and Greek, and they can choose today (because there is teaching freedom) their own preferred methods: a natural or global method, or a systematic teaching mode through all possible variations. The important thing is to respect and achieve the predetermined objectives in the official programmes.

Brocca Project

This project is named after the Public Education Ministry undersecretary who coordinated the commission in 1988. Its aim was initially to renew the programmes for the first two years of the upper secondary school, and then in 1991 for the last three years as well: in other words to redefine the whole upper secondary school system. The work of the commission defined all pedagogical details in teaching and learning, focusing at all times on the learners. The details were completed in 1994 and from that date some schools have experimented with the Brocca courses: about 761 institutions started the first experiment of which 578 were of the *Liceo Classico,* or *Liceo Scientifico* type. Some were institutions formerly known as the *Istituto Magistrale*, whose curriculum until 2000/1 had four years (and one integrative year to complete), and these have been brought into line with other schools after the Brocca Project, becoming the *Liceo Socio-Psico-Pedagogico* with a five-year curriculum like all upper secondary schools.

The Brocca Commission introduced a new weekly timetable, as you can see in the relevant tables below. All subject syllabuses (such as Latin and

Ancient Greek) paid attention for the first time to the didactic-pedagogical environment, and they describe general aims for teaching and learning with specific objectives, and suggestions for didactic tools, as well as tests and assessments.

All the Brocca programmes are available at MIUR (*Ministero dell'Istruzione, dell'Università e della Ricerca*), whose website is at www.istruzione.it or from the EDSCUOLA website, www.edscuola.it

The modern secondary system

The Italian modern secondary system is the result of numerous reforms in the last 200 years. In 1859 Minister Casati reorganised the secondary school system into the following pattern:

five years – *Gymnasium*

three years – lyceum.

Latin was taught for the whole eight years in this curriculum. Then Minister Bottai in 1940 modified the preceding partition into:

three years unified in *Scuola Media inferiore*

two years – *Gymnasium*

three years – lyceum.

Latin was taught for the whole seven years in this curriculum until 1962, and then for a total of five from 1977.

For a long time the *Liceo Classico* was the highest-level upper training institution, and here Latin and Ancient Greek were fundamental subjects in the curriculum. This type of education was the oldest in Italian schools, and it continued for a long time with a lot of students. It was followed in 1923 by new institutions such as the *Liceo Scientifico* and the *Istituto Magistrale* (Magistral Institute). Both of these had Latin as a subject on the curriculum but not as a fundamental one. These were both created by Minister Gentile.

Today in Italy schools are organised as follows:

- five years of primary school,
- three years of lower secondary school,
- five years of upper secondary school.

Initially public upper secondary education was divided into humanistic studies and technical studies. In previous times humanistic studies had many students, but in the last few decades numerous new scholastic institutions have been created to satisfy new requirements in the professional and technical world and these recruit a large number of students. In southern Italy up to 20% of upper secondary students still choose the *Liceo Classico*, but in the north it is only about 8%.

The first year in the upper secondary school has to be completed by age 15, but in 2005 a reform was drawn up by Minister Moratti, so other innovations are being introduced in the Italian system from 2006/7 (see below).

Latin, Greek and Ancient Civilisation in the secondary school system

In Italy today Latin is taught in many different schools, but Ancient Greek is taught only in the *Liceo Classico*. In all cases curricula and programmes are centralised. Latin and Greek are distinct subjects and they are not treated together, as in some other European school systems, as Classical Civilisation. Ancient Greek is taught in a normal *Liceo Classico*, and also in the experimental *Liceo Classico* (Brocca).

The number of hours for the teaching of Ancient Greek is as follows:

age	class	Ordinary lyceum	Brocca
14	1st	4	4
15	2nd	4	4
16	3rd	3	3
17	4th	3	3
18	5th	3	3

There are many variations in the teaching of Latin but there are four training fields. The Classical section is available in a normal *Liceo Classico* and experimental Brocca lyceum. In the following tables the different weekly allocation of periods is shown:

age	class	Ordinary lyceum	Brocca
14	1st	5	4
15	2nd	5	4
16	3rd	4	4
17	4th	4	4
18	5th	4	4

The Scientific section is available in an ordinary *Liceo Scientifico*, experimental Brocca lyceum and international option lyceum. In the following table the different weekly allocation of periods is shown:

age	class	Ordinary lyceum	Brocca
14	1st	4	4
15	2nd	5	4
16	3rd	4	3
17	4th	4	3
18	5th	3	3

The institutions known as *Istituto Magistrale* were originally teacher training colleges for primary school teachers, but in 2000/1 they were all transformed into new institutions, becoming experimental Brocca lyceums teaching mainly social sciences with some specialised education, technology and language courses (*Liceo delle Scienze Sociali, Liceo Linguistico, Liceo Socio-Psico-Pedagogico* and *Liceo Scientifico Tecnologico*). Latin continues to be taught for between two and four periods a week in these institutions. The linguistic section is divided into a linguistic lyceum (only in private schools) and state linguistic schools. There are some other schools (Proteo schools, International or European schools) where Latin and Greek are also taught.

Programmes

In Italy Latin and Greek (as all subjects) are regulated by ministerial programmes formulated long ago and modified at different times. The most important changes are the new programmes of Latin and Greek in the lower secondary school (*Scuola Media Inferiore*, three years from 11 to 13 years of age) in 1965, 1967 and 1991 (Brocca) and the total abolition of Latin as a curriculum subject and of the Latin examination, which was mandatory to enter the old *Liceo Classico* at this school level.

The general outline of the programmes is drawn up by the Ministry of Education which establishes a set of objectives for each subject to be studied year by year in school, such as morphology and syntax, the most important authors and their works for each class of Latin and Greek. These are fixed by MIUR, on which the Italian education system depends. The most innovative programmes are at present the Brocca programmes which date from 1991: for the first time in secondary school they have put more emphasis on educational aims, on specific objectives of knowledge and competence, and on practical methods and didactic elements in learning and teaching activities rather than only on the content which students must know. However, the take-up for the Brocca courses is quite low because they add further subjects to the curriculum and raise the total number of weekly hours.

These are the details of the government programmes for the ordinary *Liceo Classico* and ordinary *Liceo Scientifico*.

Liceo Classico

Latin: until 1967, the first year of *Liceo Classico* completed the learning of morphology and syntax and studied as authors, first, Caesar, Sallust, Ovid and Tibullus; and then, in the second year, Cicero and Virgil (*Aeneid*, Book 1). After 1967 reading of texts had to be more adapted to the age of students so teachers have greater freedom now in their selection of works.

For the three last classes (three years) in *Liceo Classico* the following programmes are fixed:
- 3rd year: literature from origins to Caesar; authors: Virgil, Caesar or Sallust, Cicero.

- 4th year: literature from Caesar to the Augustan period; authors: Lucretius, Catullus, Horace, Cicero or Livy.
- 5th year: literature from Tiberius to the fifth century; authors: Tacitus, Seneca or St Augustine, Plautus or Terence; metric rules.

Greek:

- 1st year of *Liceo Classico*: fixed elementary morphology and syntax.
- 2nd year: complete morphology and syntax.

For the three final classes (three years) in the *Liceo Classico* the programmes are fixed:

- 3rd year: literature from origins to Pindar; authors: Homer (one book) and historic works.
- 4th year: literature: Attic period; authors: lyric poets and Plato.
- 5th year: literature: Hellenistic period; one tragedy and one oration.

Ordinary Liceo Scientifico

Latin:

- 1st year: fixed elementary morphology and syntax.
- 2nd year: complete morphology and syntax, especially syntax of cases.

For the three final classes (three years) the programmes are fixed:

- 3rd year: verb and period syntax; literature: from origins to the archaic period; authors: Caesar, Catullus or Ovid.
- 4th year: literature: the period of Caesar and Cicero to the Augustan period; authors: a selection from Virgil, Horace, Sallust, Livy, Tacitus, Pliny, Seneca.
- 5th year: literature: from the Tiberian period to the end of Roman Empire; authors: Cicero, Lucretius; metric rules.

Moratti Reform

In 2003 a new law was passed, known as *Delega al Governo per la definizione delle norme generali sull'istruzione e dei livelli essenziali delle prestazioni in materia di istruzione e di formazione professionale*, which to be operative had to be implemented by decrees and guidelines. The final document that resulted is the '*Schema di Decreto*' approved on 27 May 2005.

As far as secondary schools are concerned, this reform institutes that the second education cycle, from 14 to 18 years of age, a total of five study years, can be followed in two ways:

- *istruzione secondaria di 2° grado*, depending on the Central Government
- *istruzione e formazione professionale*, depending on the regions

This reform, which started up in 2006/7, establishes the 2+2+1 system (i.e. first two years, second two years, one final year) in the upper secondary school (first two years: 14 to 15 years of age, second two years: 16 to 17 years, last year, orientation training to university/professions: 18-year-old students).

Upper secondary institutions have been denominated as *Licei* and have been divided into eight specialities:

artistico (artistic)
classico (classical)
economico (economic)
linguistico (linguistic)
musicale e coreutico (music and theatre arts)
scientifico (scientific)
tecnologico (technological)
scienze umane (social sciences).

The effect on Classical subjects is that Latin and Ancient Greek will continue together in the *Liceo Classico*, and Latin will continue also in *Liceo Linguistico*, *Scientifico* and *Scienze Umane* with a small reduction in curriculum as can be seen in the following:

Liceo Classico	1st year	2nd year	3rd year	4th year	5th year
Latin language and culture	4	4	4	4	4
Greek language and culture	4	4	3	3	3
Liceo Linguistico	1st year	2nd year	3rd year	4th year	5th year
Latin language and culture	3	3	-	-	-
Liceo delle Scienze Umane	1st year	2nd year	3rd year	4th year	5th year
Latin language and culture	3	3	2	2	-
Liceo Scientifico	1st year	2nd year	3rd year	4th year	5th year
Latin language and culture	3	3	2	2	-

If you compare the old week plan (see above, p. 73) you will note that in the *Liceo Classico* Latin has been reduced to four hours (as in Brocca courses) and not five hours as in the old plans, while in the *Liceo Scientifico* it has been further limited to a maximum of two or three hours for four years only and has been removed completely from the last year. The configuration of the new *Liceo delle Scienze Umane* is the same as that of the *Liceo Scientifico*. All this implies a reduction of the importance accorded to the Classical subjects, although they continue to retain a presence.

From 2004 MIUR commissions have defined in different steps the national OSA (*Obiettivi Specifici d'Apprendimento*, specific learning objectives) for schools, and we note that Classical subjects have been indicated as *Latin Language and Culture,* and *Greek Language and Culture.* For this programme, documents (the latest in May 2005) have been published for each discipline, setting out the knowledge and abilities which all students must obtain in these subjects, the areas to be covered in greater depth and the mandatory and/or optional sections which all students must select.

These are the expected *competences* which students must acquire for Latin in the first two years of *Liceo Classico* (14 to 15 years old).

Students must be able to:

- read texts correctly
- know how to use a dictionary
- use vocabulary correctly
- recognise syntactic, morphologic and lexical structures
- make comparisons with Latin, Greek and Italian, etc.
- recognise Latin cultural elements in studied texts
- understand and translate texts of gradual complexity (poetry or prose) independently
- complete projects and their own research about Latin language and culture with ICT tools.

Further details on the MIUR website, www.istruzione.it.

Methodology of Classics teaching

For centuries Classics had been taught in a traditional way, focusing all the attention on language study. The priority continued to be the study of grammar – all morphology and all syntax in Latin or Ancient Greek. The aim was to read and analyse selected texts (whole works or selections) in the original language in a gradual way, year by year, in the curriculum of secondary higher schools (as indicated in the tables above) until the pupils were ready to take an examination in the complete works of the most important authors. So students' tasks were to read correctly Latin and Ancient Greek texts, to memorise verbs and name inflections, to analyse the grammatical components of texts (all rules of morphology and syntax), and to translate texts correctly.

Only in the later twentieth century after different changes and reforms, from about 1970 onwards, did people start to pay particular attention to text and context together, as well as to the grammatical side of Classical Studies. That continues to be important in the first two years of higher secondary education, but it is not the only aspect studied. Therefore, from 1980 different theories and methodologies were introduced into Italy from other European countries, but the 'centrality of the text' continued to be considered by many teachers to be the fundamental point of entry to Classical cultures through original works. Consequently, in 1990 the Brocca Project (see above) attempted to put this theory into practice through experimental courses.

Teachers continue to be able to choose the methodologies they want to use in their daily classroom teaching, so as a result we find in our country that many teachers apply traditional teaching methods, while others use more innovative and experimental methods. We also find a large number of different course books that propose various learning systems, but all must make clear that they will teach towards the most important aims and objectives that students must obtain in Classical subjects, as established by the MIUR documents.

Assessment

Teachers must evaluate the learning of students in Latin and Ancient Greek at almost all levels through periodic checks and tests that are generally divided between oral and written tests. Only a few levels have oral examinations and then in a few experimental courses only. Ministerial documents suggest that an extensive number of tests be taken in every term of the school year (normally three orals and three written) to verify the learning progress of students and to assess specific objectives. Each school is able to decide the criteria to attribute specific marks for each level in each subject: in Italy a decimal system from one to ten is used in higher secondary schools, with six as the minimum pass mark.

Oral examinations generally consist of a dialogue between candidate and teacher in which the students must show that they:
- are able to read correctly,
- are familiar with the original language,
- know the language system,
- can analyse and translate correctly,
- can connect everything to a specific cultural context.

Over the years new types of tests have been introduced, which always derive from the modern language systems (such as quizzes in different modes: multiple-choice answers, Cloze tests, and so on. The Cloze test measures students' comprehension abilities by giving them a short text, with blanks where some of the words should be, and asking them to fill in the blanks. However, the traditional written translation test is still mandatory for almost all levels in the curriculum and it consists generally of a Latin or Ancient Greek text (appropriate to the learning level of students) to be translated correctly into Italian.

Final examination

Final examinations were introduced for the first time in 1923 (to test all subjects in the curriculum) and were reformed for the first time in 1969 (introducing only two written tests and oral tests for just two subjects). Then the examinations were reformed again with some variations from 1997 to 2003, and the last changes introduced, leaving three written tests and one oral multidisciplinary test. Latin and Ancient Greek are part of the core curriculum only in the *Liceo Classico*, so at the final examination students must demonstrate their learning in these subjects with a written test, generally Latin or Ancient Greek in alternate years, which always consists of a text to translate into Italian (its typology has not been changed in years!). This is the second test because the first examination is in Italian Language and Literature and this is taken by all students in all schools; it is centralised and sent to schools directly by MIUR. Students must work for a maximum of four hours and can use only a Latin or Ancient Greek Dictionary. The structure of the second test is the same every year, with a selection of different authors and works. Then there is a written multidisciplinary test, the third test (freely set internally by the teachers' councils in every school), and as the last test the final '*collo-quium*', an oral multidisciplinary discussion.

Each written test is marked or evaluated on a scale of zero to a maximum of 15 credit points (they total 45 because there are three written tests); the oral test is marked out of 35 points and students can also have a maximum of 20 points for all personal coursework. So the final mark is expressed as a percentage as the marks add up to 100.

Course books and dictionaries

In Italy there are many manuals or course books to teach Latin and Ancient Greek, based on different teaching and learning methodologies. Each teacher can choose the best tool for his or her daily work in the class-room and for students learning at home.

Until the 1970s, teachers had only a few traditional manuals, with descriptive grammar and exercises limited to translations of phrases, or they had complete versions of various authors. For a long time most of the students in Italy learned the grammar of the Classical languages for their first two years with the following manuals:

- for Latin: V. Tantucci, *Urbis et Orbis Lingua*, Poseidonia Edit.
- for Ancient Greek: A. Sivieri and P. Vivian, *Grammatica ed Esercizi Greci*, G. D'Anna Edit.

After the innovations in secondary high schools from about 1970 to 1980 numerous manuals were published, more or less innovative but really more adapted to the needs of the new learning and teaching methods, with different types of exercises, and generally closer to the learning approaches of modern languages. The AIE (*Associazione Italiana Editori*) published in 2005 the following list of Classics manuals which are used most in Italy:

Latin:
Grammar: *Biennium* (students 14 to 15 years old):
N. Flocchini, P. Guidotti Bacci and M. Moscio, *Nuovo Comprendere e Tradurre*, Ed. Bompiani
A. Diotti, *Nova Lexis*, Ed. B. Mondadori
Latin literature: *Triennium* (students 16 to 18 years old):
G. Garbarino, *Opera*, Ed. Paravia
G.B. Conte, *Corso Integrato di Letteratura Latina*, Ed. Le Monnier

Ancient Greek:
Grammar: *Biennium* (students 14 to 15 years old):
C. Campanini and P. Scaglietti, *Greco*, Ed. Sansoni
L. Bottin and S. Quaglia, *Lingua Greca*, Ed. Minerva Italica
Ancient Greek Literature: *Triennium* (students 16 to 18 years old):
M. Casertano and G. Nuzzo, *Storia e Testi della Letteratura Greca*, Ed. Palumbo
L. Rossi and R. Nicolai, *Storia e Testi della Letteratura Greca*, Ed. Le Monnier

Dictionaries are the other fundamental tools for teaching and learning Classics and for many years the panorama of dictionaries in Italian schools was limited to a few names. Today the most widely used are:

IL (Latin-Italian; Italian-Latin Dictionary) by L. Castiglioni and S. Mariotti, Ed. Loescher, also CD-ROM
Nuovo Vocabolario (Latin-Italian; Italian-Latin Dictionary) by Campanini and Carboni, Ed. Paravia
Vocabolario Greco Italiano (Greek-Italian Dictionary) by L. Rocci, Ed. D. Alighieri
GI (Greek-Italian Dictionary) by F. Montanari, Ed. Loescher, also CD-ROM
Il dizionario della lingua latina, by G.B. Conte, E. Pianezzola and G. Ranucci, Ed. Le Monnier

Conclusion

Since 1969 Latin has no longer been the subject of a final examination in the *Liceo Scientifico*, which has significantly reduced the importance of the subject in the eyes of the students and of some teachers. As the same teacher in the *Liceo Scientifico* teaches both the Italian mother tongue and Latin the two subjects have become closely linked.

The reforms introduced over recent years have effectively reduced the timetable allowance and the importance previously assigned to Greek and Latin. The demands on the students of learning the Classical languages require a substantial commitment of time and effort which seems to many to be disproportionate. Consequently it has become necessary to find methods of reducing the contents and new ways of teaching. However, many aspects of the ancient Roman world are immediate and obvious to young people in Italy and this remains an important element in their culture, even though less emphasis is placed now in school on the intricacies of Latin grammar.

Latvia

Vita Paparinska and Gita Berzina

In Latvia Classics teaching was an integral part of the traditional school and university education system until the introduction of the uniform Soviet educational system. In the 1940s Classical languages were abolished from the school curricula. In the 1950s the changes affected Classics at the university level and the only programme of Classical Philology in Latvia (offered by the University of Latvia) was closed. Although the Latin language course was retained in the Humanities programmes and all the students of Humanities read some ancient literature, the closing of the programme of Classical Philology meant a real danger to the development and even the existence of Classics as a branch of scholarship. No new Classicists in Latvia were being trained and Classics could possibly have disappeared gradually from the university programmes.

The 1990s brought significant changes to Latvia and its place in the world. In general terms, this meant an increased appreciation of our common European cultural heritage, and greater awareness of the existence of continuing cultural values and of the role of this cultural heritage in the formation and development of the European culture of which Latvia forms a part. By perceiving themselves as individuals with a specific historical and cultural background, people began to look with a new understanding and interest at the history of their nation, their country and humanity in general. The political changes were the decisive factor in bringing about the general shift of interest to the specific historical and cultural background of the nation. Respect for the individual and acceptance of diversity as a part of normal life created favourable conditions for the liberalisation of the education system.

The major impact of this change was the renewal of the programme of Classical Philology at the University of Latvia and the introduction and expansion of the study of the Classical world in those schools which were willing and ready to take this on. As the school authorities were granted the authority to develop a system of optional courses as a supplement to the mandatory courses required by the national curriculum, Classics could be reintroduced into the school curriculum if the relevant school authorities made this decision. Consequently, Classics in the 1990s enjoyed great popularity in the eyes of the general public and the media. Studying Classics was 'the thing to do' – it was considered to be modern, elitist and a little exotic. A number of schools made an attempt to start a new model of education, which would include the Classical languages and non-linguistic Classics courses. It was a challenge after 40 years of interruption in the tradition of training Classical teachers, as there were few Classics teachers available. The schools were lucky if they found a teacher who had studied the Latin language for a year or two as a supplement to his or her major study area. Therefore, the schools generally had to narrow the idea of Classics down to a non-linguistic, fragmentary Classics teaching model where different aspects of the Classical world were studied within a wider course: history, literature, philosophy, culture, etc. This model continues to predominate in schools up to the present.

Now, a little more than ten years after political independence was regained and after a year as a member state of the European Union, the attitude of the general public to cultural values has changed somewhat. The economic situation has brought about at government level a more utilitarian and pragmatic world understanding. The media contribute to this tendency. In all spheres of life those areas that promise most economic benefit are promoted and praised – foremost the modern technologies and economics. Sound educational policy and long-term strategy are non-existent. Ultimately, education seems to be a minor consideration in the everyday work of the government. In relation to education, the favourite leading concept of the government is 'market requirements'. Humanities are regarded as 'of no practical value' and are more or less ignored.

The attitude of the general public now concerning Classics can be characterised as ignorance, indifference or amazed surprise that such an 'exotic' area of scholarship still exists and is studied at different levels. The most obvious questions to Classicists are: 'What do we need Classics for?' or 'What kind of job can you get with a Classics education?' This is a direct result of the interrupted tradition of Classical education, as Classical texts have not been read in Latvia for about 50 years, and more than a whole generation has grown up without an idea of what Classics represents. Parents who have not read Classics, especially the Classical languages, do not and cannot persuade their children that Classics is fascinating and useful from the practical point of view as well: a person with some knowledge of Latin or Greek can understand the functioning of his or her mother tongue better and consequently, by seeing similarities in language structure, can learn modern languages more easily. This is a pity as the Classical languages, especially Latin, could be instrumental in learning the most important modern languages in Latvia – English, French, German and Russian.

The negative attitude towards Classics is not so severe within the Ministry of Education as within the general public. After all, the Ministry officials are all university graduates and many of them have read the Classical languages or non-linguistic Classics courses at some point in their educational careers. The Ministry is more academically oriented than the government, and consequently its attitude to Classics is more

understanding and benevolent, at least in words. However, the verbal attitude is one thing and practical measures taken to support Classics are
something else. Unfortunately in most cases, when Classics teachers deal
with officials, they can expect only verbal support.

Classicists receive no support from the media in respect to Classics
teaching. On the whole the media rarely deal with educational issues, and
Classics in the context of education is not discussed. Somewhat more
attention is paid by the media to the cultural news aspect of the Classics –
some information is occasionally provided about the new translations/
publications of Classical texts and other scholarly activities related to
Classics, but only in specific cultural publications or in the general
cultural sections of the press. This happens comparatively rarely, and thus
the news related to Classics is dissolved in the wide and varied stream of
information.

It is our opinion that ministry officials, school directors and even
university academic leaders and administrators do not always fully understand the objective of Classics teaching and the importance of the
knowledge and understanding of the ancient world for any student, no
matter what his or her professional career may be. Classics is often
regarded as a very narrow, highly specialised, elitist area of scholarship,
which has little or even no practical application in the modern world. Still
the senior officials vaguely perceive that Classics is something that any
educational system should include, and at appropriate moments they take
pride in speaking of 'our classical academic education', 'our classical tradition of education', 'our classical universities' and 'our classical schools'.
This delicate balance between insufficient understanding and intuitive
appreciation of the value of Classics has helped to preserve Classical
languages and the non-linguistic Classics courses in the system of education, although at times the position of Classics is very precarious.

At first glance the impression is that Classics in the school education
system is fairly well represented. Students in high school have the opportunity to study different aspects of Classics – ancient history, ancient
philosophy, Classical culture, and ancient literature – as part of more
general courses. Sometimes the school also offers the Latin language
course. However, the students often leave school with an insufficient and
superficial knowledge of antiquity and its cultural heritage.

There are two reasons for this incongruity – the possibility of studying
different aspects of Classics and the inadequate results. First there is the
poor organisation of Classics teaching, and second, the lack of professional
Classics teachers. The reason for the poor organisation of Classics
teaching is the current structure of the school syllabus. In primary schools
all the courses are obligatory. The syllabus of high schools includes both
the obligatory and optional courses. The obligatory courses are mother
tongue and literature, mathematics, history, computer science, and one
foreign language. A number of the courses offered to high school students

are optional and they may select courses from a wide range of those offered. The selection of the optional courses chosen reveals two marked tendencies. One of them – and a positive one – shows that students are interested in those courses of Humanities which provide knowledge of the general European cultural environment and the Classical heritage: history of culture, philosophy, and history of world literature. The other tendency – and this is the dominant one – displays the role of the utilitarian motivation, where students select those courses which may be useful for their future professional careers: economics, marketing, political science, and modern languages.

As the optional courses generally are not structured into branches related to a particular curriculum area, the students often select them chaotically. Thus the result of the students' choice may fail to produce an overall coherent picture of any area and it may present only fragmentary incomplete impressions. This is especially evident in relation to the ancient world. The Humanities-related courses definitely include an overview of the relevant area of the ancient world. This is, of course, on the one hand very good, as students see the ancient world and its heritage as the basis for further development of scholarship and culture. On the other hand, generally the time allotted to the ancient world is quite short, and so the students obtain only a superficial knowledge. However, the major problem is that high school students are not able to develop a complete picture of the Classical world from the different aspects they read in the different courses. Besides, if the students do not select all the courses which include an overview of an aspect of the ancient world, important areas of study will remain missing.

Still worse is the situation with the teaching of Classical languages. Greek is not offered in any of the high schools of Latvia. Latin language as an optional course is offered in a few schools. These schools are mostly *Gymnasia* and Humanities-oriented schools, and even there the Latin language is offered on an equal basis with many other optional courses. This is, of course, a disadvantageous situation for Latin, as it is competing with other courses that many students and their parents consider to be more closely related to the modern world. Thus the number of students who study Latin is quite small – about 300 students annually. These are students aged 15 to 18 as Latin is offered only in high schools. The students read only Classical Latin, generally using the revised pronunciation.

Most often the duration of the Latin language course is one or two years and consists of one or two classes per week. The course focuses on language studies and the development of translation skills. In the first study year the students cover most of the grammar material and regularly work with translation of texts adjusted to the relevant grammar theme. Those who opt to take a second year of Latin can pass over to reading extracts from authentic texts. The first prose authors the students read are Caesar and Cicero, and from poetry Virgil, Horace, Ovid and Catullus.

The selection of the Latin language textbook is the responsibility of the teacher. There are a number of textbooks available, and all of them are structured according to the traditional method of teaching – with a sound grammatical base, which is supplemented and illustrated by adapted texts or by sentences and extracts from authentic texts. The selection of texts is quite extensive, and the contents provide ample opportunities for the teacher to comment on the particular aspect of the Classical world under consideration. There are a couple of textbooks with fragments exclusively of authentic texts available, but school students find it more interesting to read a piece of text that deals specifically with some aspect of the ancient world, and the authenticity of the text, at least at the beginning of studies, is not of primary importance to them.

Although the contents of the Latin textbooks in most cases are quite satisfactory, often they are visually not very attractive because they have been in use for a long time. Only one textbook and a short Latin grammar for students whose mother tongue is Latvian have been published during the last ten years. For students whose mother tongue is Russian, the situation is better – updated Latin textbooks, grammar books and dictionaries are published regularly in Russia and can be purchased there.

One of the biggest challenges for Latin language teaching is the lack of uniform official requirements for the course contents and final examination. Although the teachers are obliged to follow the Latin language standard set by the Ministry of Education, this standard envisages a one-year course and thus uniformity of requirements works only for the first year of Latin language teaching. The content of the second and third year of the course depends on the level of knowledge of students who have selected Latin and the ideas of the teacher about the most suitable approach to further language teaching. Unfortunately, owing to the small number of students who select Latin, it is not one of the courses for which the Ministry of Education has developed a uniform final test. Thus the evaluation of the results of the Latin language course is the responsibility solely of the teacher. The final test usually includes translation of an unseen text with the help of a dictionary and the teacher may ask the students to answer some grammar questions. This lack of an officially recognised final test in Latin has a negative impact on people's attitude to the course, as it creates an impression that Latin is not important enough to compete with other courses at the level of the final assessment.

Another reason for the students' vague understanding of the Classical world is the problem of teachers. There are not enough Classical Philologists available for teaching jobs at schools as the annual number of graduates with a BA degree in Classical Philology is small, at about only ten persons per year. Even if the school obtains such a specialist it cannot offer him or her a full-time job owing to the small number of lessons available. Thus the teaching of the Latin language is an additional responsibility of a teacher, usually a non-specialist, whose major area is mother tongue and literature or English. Because of this insufficient number of Classical Philology specialists who could go to schools, it is not realistic to make strong demands to the Ministry of Education about making Latin a mandatory course in schools.

The conclusion regarding the situation of Classics teaching in schools is that although Classics constitutes a part of every student's education, it can be a very insignificant part, for two reasons. First, most of the courses, which include an overview of the Classical world from the relevant course aspect, are optional; and, secondly, different aspects of Classics are not self-contained courses and consequently are not consolidated into one uniform course or module. Thus the teaching of different fragmented aspects does not give the students a uniform picture of the Classical world.

Classics teaching in the university education system likewise has its challenges, and in many ways they are identical to those of the school system and are a direct result of Classics teaching in schools. However, unlike the school system, in universities the tradition of Classics teaching has not been interrupted (although within the Soviet education system it was limited). At present, depending on the programme, Classics is represented in the university system by the Classical languages and/or non-linguistic Classics courses – ancient literature, ancient philosophy, ancient history, mythology, Roman law, ancient culture.

The most comprehensive picture of the Classical world is provided by the programme of Classical Philology. This programme in Latvia is offered by only one university – the University of Latvia. The programme of Classical Philology has defined its objective as to provide sufficient knowledge of the Latin and Greek languages and translation skills in order to enable the student to read authentic Classical texts and understand their role and significance within the framework of the literary culture of the Classical world and for further development of literature in the modern world. The contents of the programme of Classical Philology ensure that it can and does reach this goal. Each course which forms a part of the comparatively wide programme focuses on a separate aspect of the Classical world and they all come together to create comprehensive understanding that the Classical heritage is the foundation of the modern cultural environment.

Admission of students to the programme of Classical Philology is competitive – generally there are about eight applicants per slot. Replies to questionnaires filled in by the new undergraduates show that their motivation for selecting the programme of Classical Philology is an interest in the cultural heritage of the ancient world, especially literature. Obviously Classics teaching in schools, although fragmentary, has managed to excite the interest of students (at least some of them!) in the Classical world. Still the analysis of the questionnaires and of the educational background of the new undergraduate students of the programme of Classical Philology reveals some disturbing tendencies. During more than ten years of the existence of the programme of Classical Philology only one undergraduate student had prior knowledge of Latin (a rough estimate would be one out of about 300 undergraduates). This shows that the Latin language course at schools is not very inspiring or motivating for further studies of Classics at university level and those students who were interested in Classics did not have the opportunity to study the Classical languages at school. Thus for the undergraduate students of Classical Philology the first contact with the Classical languages is within the framework of the university programme. Besides, owing to the fragmented and uneven general knowledge of the Classical world within the student group the undergraduate programme provides the first serious insight into the cultural heritage of antiquity.

A major challenge for the Elementary Latin and Elementary Greek courses is the course content. The undergraduate students read the non-linguistic Classics courses – ancient literature, ancient history, ancient culture and mythology – concurrently with the Classical languages or later. Therefore, many of the facts and notions related to the Classical world which the students encounter in the Latin language course require additional comment and explanation. For this reason and in view of the brevity of the undergraduate programme, Elementary Latin and Elementary Greek are not offered as a separate entity. The exact opposite is the case. For a successful implementation of the programme, right from the first lesson grammar is supplemented with an insight into the cultural environment. This method has certain drawbacks as sometimes there is not enough time for a more detailed study of some grammar themes. Still the main advantage is that the language classes are more interesting and they awaken the students' interest in different aspects of the ancient world. Moreover, the students see from the very beginning the indispensable role of language in studying and understanding the Classical heritage.

This problem of the teaching of Classical languages and the scope and content of the course was aggravated in the academic year 2004/5 when the University of Latvia started the transition from a four-year to a three-year undergraduate programme. The condensed time period is a challenge for the programme of Classical Philology, as the students in three years have to learn two completely new languages – Latin and Greek – and read at least the minimum of authentic ancient texts that will enable them students to appreciate the literary heritage of the ancient world. As the first study year is dedicated to reading elementary Latin and Greek, only two years remain for advanced study of the languages and reading of the authentic texts. The academic staff of the Department of Classical Philology have always been rather reserved about studying ancient literature only or mainly from translations. In the four-year undergraduate programme a satisfactory balance had been reached – students read extensive fragments of the authentic text of most of the major literary works and these readings were supplemented by the study of the whole texts in translations. The situation is different with the new three-year undergraduate programme, as it is not realistic to expect that the students will be able to read the same amount of authentic texts. This has been the reason for reconsidering the content of the programme of Classical Philology and the balance between authentic texts and translations. Unfortunately in future more emphasis will have to be placed on translations.

The transition to the three-year undergraduate programmes has had a serious impact on all the university programmes. Shortening a programme inevitably leads to a reduction of the course duration and content. First of all, these changes affect courses with a supplementary status in the programme. The Classics Faculty is mainly concerned about the new status of their relevant courses (the languages and the non-linguistic Classics courses) in those programmes where Classics courses have traditionally been mandatory. These are the programmes of History, Philosophy, Theology, Law, Education and Philology.

In the above-mentioned programmes the courses of the Classical languages have been considerably reduced. Presently the best option for a Classicist who is teaching Latin or Greek to the students of these programmes is to teach the course for one year (two semesters) with one class per week or for four months (one semester) with two classes per week. It is a considerable challenge to structure the course in an appropriate way so that the students feel they have learned something valuable and useful for their selected branch of scholarship. Besides, the course may become very dull if the teacher concentrates mainly or only on the language and grammar facts without a wider context of the relevant texts the students are reading. No matter how short the Classical language course is, the teacher must find time for the commentary from the perspective of the Classical heritage as through this the Classical language course comes alive. Of course, the additional information provided by the teacher must not surpass the language studies. In addition, as the Classical language course is supplementary to the major study area, the students gain knowledge of the historical/cultural/intellectual background within which the language functions in their major courses.

Finally we would like to mention an initiative that the staff of the Department of Classical Philology began a couple of years ago. In response to the remarks and reprimands, both public and private, of the highest academic authorities in the University of Latvia that the programme of Classical Philology was too small, too expensive, too elitist and actually of interest to very few people (meaning – what do we need Classics for in our modern world?), the teachers opened up the entry to general Elementary Latin and Elementary Greek courses to any student of the University. The response exceeded our wildest imaginings, as the number of applicants was much bigger than could be accommodated. It was somewhat disappointing that about half of the applicants did not pursue their interest in the Classical languages further after the first class, but those who did remain continued their studies with much motivation and interest. And the results, when working with students with very different educational backgrounds, who were doing something they really enjoyed, were very good. Some students started reading authentic Latin texts after four months of study and serious authentic Greek texts in a year.

We think this is a telling fact. The values of the Classical world are eternal, and people strive for them. People want to know and understand the Classical heritage as the foundation of the European culture in the widest sense, the common European heritage that enables any individual to feel a sense of belonging to the European family. Looking back to the Classical values does not mean that we are looking at the long-forgotten past. Cicero was aware that without the knowledge of the past there is no future and only the past provides the understanding of one's place in the historical sequence (*Orator* 120). We can only agree with him. Classics is the tool that helps us to understand the present and look forward to the future.

The Netherlands

Egge Tijsseling

A teacher of Classics in the Netherlands will be found working at either a grammar school or a *Gymnasium* or in one of the many comprehensive schools where Latin and sometimes Greek are taught. There are 40 *Gymnasia* in the country. This type of school has compulsory Latin for the pupils aged 12, compulsory Greek and Latin for the pupils aged 13 and 14, and Latin and/or Greek for the last three years, when their ages range from 15 to 17 or 18.

The subjects Latin and Greek cover almost anything as long as it is Classical: language, the Classical world, history, literature, and so on. For the cultural aspects of Classics a separate subject has been developed in the Netherlands: KCV (*Klassieke Culturele Vorming*) or Classical Cultural Education. For all pupils learning Latin or Greek this subject is compulsory in their fourth year (when they are aged 15 or 16). They take this subject every week, for two or three periods of 50 minutes each, during one academic year. KCV deals with the mythology, art, architecture and sculpture of antiquity, and its appreciation and reception through the ages. The pupils learn, for example, to compare ancient and modern paintings of a mythological subject, to become familiar with the function of Roman or Greek temples, and to understand the function of a theatre in ancient and modern times. Such a study might involve, for example, Jean Anouilh's treatment of Sophocles' *Antigone*, showing how he adapted the story to illustrate the position of the French people under Nazi occupation. Some teachers have expressed concern that KCV might be a Trojan horse which would undermine the teaching of the Classical languages. This worry does not appear to have been borne out in practice and many teachers report enthusiastic responses from pupils.

In most lessons of Classical languages too there is some cultural element such as archaeology, art or philosophy. These non-linguistic aspects of Classics will be introduced according to which authors are being read. Teaching other subjects, modern languages, for instance, is not within the competence of Classics specialists. The only other thing they are officially allowed to do is to teach History to pupils aged 12, because History teaching generally starts chronologically. Sometimes a teacher may be asked to teach History when a school is short of History staff, and of course all teachers are allowed to teach other subjects once they have studied them. The Netherlands is suffering from an increasing shortage of teachers, and consequently headteachers often have to resort to the appointment of teachers who are not always fully qualified. This is also the case for Classics teaching, where there is a continuing shortage.

Curriculum

Teachers in the Netherlands are more or less free to choose, in consultation with their colleagues, their own subject matter for their lessons. Of course, they have to take examination requirements into account, but they are free to take their own route to arrive at the common final assessment. There may be some schools which use medieval or Neo-Latin texts as part of their reading, but the great majority stick to Classical Latin. Dutch teachers all use the *pronuntiatio restituta* for reading Latin aloud.

With reference to Greek the situation is the same. The main menu is Classical Greek, although some teachers with a command of Modern Greek may possibly use this knowledge in their lessons. In the pronunciation of Greek, accents are observed, but for stress not pitch, and the Erasmian pronunciation is followed.

Classics in the *Gymnasium*

In our country the thinking about language or non-linguistic learning is divided. The experts (teachers at schools and universities) are mainly concerned with language teaching and language learning, but the bodies that have to spend their money and time, the government and the pupils, usually tend to the direction of non-linguistic learning. The study of Classical languages requires, as we all know, a lot of hard work and devotion, and in addition the relevance of Classics to contemporary society is always a matter for debate. For these reasons the tendency is for the number of periods on the timetable to decrease, if ever there is any change. If the number of periods decreases, which in practice has happened twice in the last 35 years, some people think it is wiser to turn to non-linguistic learning and teach a variety of subjects to the pupils rather than sticking to language teaching. Some teachers who tend towards pessimism conclude as a result that it is hard to get much further than elementary grammar and some adapted texts by Caesar or Homer. On the other hand more optimistic ones look at the established place of Latin and/or Greek on the timetable of the *Gymnasium*, and in addition they know they have large classes for either of the two Classical languages to teach, and they conclude that the state of Classics teaching in the Netherlands, in comparison to some other countries, is not in such a bad state as some may imagine.

The pupils begin Latin and Greek at different ages, depending on the type of school they attend. At comprehensive schools (schools which cater for the whole ability range in separate academic levels) Classics is not compulsory. If they choose to follow these subjects, they begin Latin at the age of 13 and Greek at the age of 14. When they go to a school that offers only *Gymnasium*, they begin Latin at the age of 12 and Greek when they are 13. When they are about 18 all pupils in all schools sit the same examinations. At comprehensive schools no Latin or Greek is offered to the pupils during their first year (when they are 12). In *Gymnasia* Latin is compulsory in year 1 (when they are 12) and both Classical languages are compulsory in years 2 and 3 (when the pupils are about 13 and 14 years old). Finally one of either Latin or Greek is compulsory in the last three years (when they are 15 to 18). At comprehensive schools the pupils are free to choose Classics in their second or third year and to drop it at the end of each year.

Attitudes towards Classics

Classics can encounter real political problems. The government thinks it is not very relevant to society, although it made substantial grants to the five university Classics departments in the mid-1990s. Many who themselves did not go to a school which taught Classics regard the subject as elitist, and in addition many pupils at school think it is hard to master. The particular consequence of this is that the schools with only *Gymnasium* education are small schools, with an average of about 650 pupils. However, the *Gymnasia* with their compulsory Greek and Latin continue to be popular with Dutch parents. They like the continuing tradition of this typically Dutch education and they like the idea of the small community school which looks after its pupils individually. There appears to be little opposition to the compulsory element in the curriculum. Indeed, in Amsterdam two new *Gymnasia* have recently been opened to cope with the demand for this type of schooling. Laurien Crump examines the issues raised by the position of the *Gymnasium* in modern Dutch society and the way Classics fits into the equation in a forthcoming article (Crump in Lister, forthcoming). She looks at contemporary Latin teaching in Dutch schools, particularly the *Gymnasium,* and asks whether more can be done to make the lessons more relevant to the young people who have to take the subjects. She also examines how Latin and Greek can play a part in the move towards a more independent method of study for Dutch pupils towards the end of their education.

A result of the compulsory nature of Latin and Greek in the *Gymnasium* is that all types of student are found in the class. They tend to accept that having to do these subjects is part of the deal, but it is also true that not all of them will be actively interested in pursuing Classical subjects in depth. The personality of the teacher and the relevance he or she brings to the lesson play a vital part here in maintaining the motivation and active participation of the students. As always, having Latin as a compulsory subject, as opposed to an optional one, has its disadvantages as well as advantages. In the Dutch comprehensive school system, a student taking Latin and/or Greek would be taking more subjects than necessary which would mark the student out from the others.

When pupils have the opportunity after three years (when they are about 15) to choose Latin or Greek, most of them take Latin as their one compulsory language. Taking both languages is possible and there are some who do. The numbers can vary from at least 40% in some Amsterdam schools to only 3% or 4% in others. Some schools consider Greek more difficult than Latin and find it easier to organise Latin classes within the timetable, while others consider Latin more useful for such subjects as Law and Medicine.

At the *Gymnasia* teachers generally do not have to work hard to keep Classics on the timetable. The long tradition of Classical subjects tends to give them a steady position. At comprehensive schools things are more difficult, and because of the small numbers of pupils that choose Latin or Greek teachers have to work with combined classes. They may have to deal at the same time with pupils of different ages, different subjects, different authors, and all in the same period of a maximum of 50 minutes. Other schools may simply reduce the number of weekly lessons or ask teachers to take extra classes on top of their normal allocation.

Examinations

In the end all pupils sit the same examinations. These are a combination of on average six internal examinations set by the individual school and one externally set examination which is the same throughout the whole country. This external examination is internally assessed and externally moderated. The schools have the freedom to make up their own internal examinations, but this freedom operates within certain limits. The teacher, in discussion with colleagues in the school, is free to choose authors, for instance, but within certain genres, and there are also criteria for minimum numbers of pages to be read in Latin and Greek. The external examination is always set on a certain theme or topic in literature which has been studied in class. Recent examples of these examination themes are philosophical texts by Cicero for Latin and *The Trojan Women* by Euripides for Greek. The pupils always have to read secondary literature too for both internal and external examinations. This is collected into convenient volumes for the students which are published each year for the examination candidates. A second part of the external examination is an unseen text for translation into Dutch. This external examination mark makes up 50% of their final mark.

Between 50% and 60% of the pupils who begin Latin and Greek at the schools where at least one of the subjects is compulsory sit the final examinations. At comprehensive schools the numbers are lower, because the pupils can drop the Classical subjects more easily in the course of their school career.

Classics and modern languages

Many teachers would agree that learning Latin and Greek helps young people to learn modern languages, although this is very hard to measure. Because the pupils follow Latin or Greek, there may be fewer lessons on the timetable for modern languages according to the programme of study each student follows. For the Netherlands, English is the most important modern language; second and third are German and French. Only very few schools offer Spanish, Italian or Russian. In general it is acknowledged that the standard of modern language learning in the Netherlands is very high. The pupils' level of English is generally very good and many will have some good basic knowledge of other languages too. Most Dutch teachers of Classics will have some knowledge of Italian, for example. Therefore, some teachers may argue for the retention of Classics on the timetable because of the practical use of Latin and Greek for the learning of writing and spelling in a modern language and also in the mother tongue.

Further study and universities

Helping pupils to choose their academic study is officially the job of one or more senior teachers (*decaan* or adviser), trained to do this job. They get all the information from all the universities to help the pupils make their choice. Some Classics teachers get involved in this kind of area and take an active part in giving advice to the final-year students. This can give Classics a good profile and encourage students to continue at university. Every year about 70 students begin studying Classics at the universities of Groningen, Nijmegen, Leiden and Amsterdam (at both the University of Amsterdam and the Free University).

The universities used to train people for education or for academic work. To be allowed to work at a university it is necessary to write a doctoral thesis, but only very few complete their thesis and stay in a university post afterwards. There are a number of students who go on after their degree study of on average four years to a further year of teacher training and to a career as a professional Classics teacher. However, more students at university today are studying Classics for its own sake, and not only as an entry to teaching. They go on to a wide variety of careers after university.

Trips and extracurricular activities

Some teachers in *Gymnasia* take regular trips with their pupils to sites of

Classical interest. They frequently go with their pupils aged 16 or 17 (fifth-formers) to Rome and Florence, or to Greece or Turkey. These trips are well prepared in the preceding months. For KCV (see above) the pupils aged 15 or 16 have to go to see four plays on a Classical theme or visit four museums with exhibitions of Classical art. They have to write a report about every visit. This shows the continuing influence of Classics on contemporary culture in Holland.

Textbooks

For Latin the textbook most widely used is *Roma* (Fisser et al. 2000), which gives a sound grammatical and cultural grounding and furthermore adapted texts and language exercises. Most teachers would agree that a textbook written in another language than Dutch would not be a good idea, because the pupils already have their problems with the Latin and Greek. There is also a new edition of *Via Nova* (van Assendelft et al. 2004) and a recent publication: *Fortuna* (Hupperts et al. 2004). Both of these are currently popular with teachers and pupils.

For Greek, *Pallas* (Jans et al. 2004) is the most widely used textbook in the Netherlands. This textbook is designed more for rapid reading with grammatical exercises than for a sound grammatical grounding. There are plenty of exercises and the teacher is free to choose which ones to do and which ones to omit, depending on the specific needs of the class in question. This grounding has to be achieved for the 15-year-olds, after they have finished the textbook. The cultural part is wonderful; the texts are adapted from all kinds of Greek authors. Both textbooks, *Roma* and *Pallas*, have been in use for about eight years now and have been recently updated. *Pallas* Volume III contains an in-depth anthology of texts and exercises which is used in the higher classes. There is also a Dutch version of the JACT publication *Reading Greek* which is designed for older beginners (Jones and Sidwell 1978). This is called *Hellenike* (van der Heuvel and van Duivenboden 1995) and it is a useful alternative to *Pallas*.

The first authentic text which pupils encounter may vary: for Greek it is often Lucian, the New Testament or Herodotus; for Latin, Caesar, Ovid or Nepos. There are always problems for pupils in adapting to authentic texts, and they will usually find difficulties with word order, length of sentences, the treatment of the verbs and the constructions of the Classical languages. These days in Latin, Tacitus and comedy are considered to be too difficult, and in Greek the same applies to Aeschylus and Plato. This means that these authors and these genres are not used for the external examination, but the teacher is always free to offer them in the fifth form (pupils aged 16 to 17), adapted and with many notes.

Dutch teachers are in the unusual position for Classics teachers in Europe of having a stable situation where Latin and Greek (as well as KCV) have an assured place in the timetable of their state schools. We may offer a positive example to other countries where the subject is under greater threat, showing that the study of the Classical world, its culture and languages need not be regarded as old-fashioned and irrelevant to today's world. This academic and demanding curriculum is offered to all pupils who will benefit from it. As a result, the Netherlands does not have a private education system competing with its state system, as is the case with the UK. With good teaching and enthusiastic pupils it can be a meaningful and useful component of a forward-looking academic curriculum.

Portugal

Aires Pereira do Couto and Francisco de Oliveira

Social and political background

In Portugal the subject of Classics is highly acknowledged by the media and it can even be said that there is renewed interest in all the forms of expression that we have inherited from Greco-Roman civilisation, particularly in literature, in the historical novel and in lyric poetry, where Classical symbolism and mythology provide frequent influences and are often evoked. There is a great contemporary interest in translations of Classical texts, especially plays, but also in history and epics as well. This interest is also noticeable in the names of businesses and products, and in advertising campaigns, such as the names *Optimus* and *Vobis* in the telecommunications and information technology sectors.

However, this cultural presence does not correspond to any permanent and continuous initiative favouring a policy of obligatory, or at least expanded, teaching of the Classical languages. Some public stances by intellectuals in favour of the teaching of Latin, especially for future specialists in modern languages, history, philosophy and law, seem almost to take the form of laments, which are hardly effective at the policy-making level. What seems most obvious is that everything is cooked up by Portuguese bureaucrats with their community partners in technical meetings in Brussels, or even in Delphi.

In addition, in Portugal there is no official perception that Classics is a European discipline, and this situation has not changed in the last 20 years. It is true that 'our civilisation' is frequently spoken about, more, in fact, than Western and European values are, which bring together ideas such as democracy and human dignity; but this discourse is not immediately directed at questions of European identity, and still less at the creation of a curriculum which would include instruction in the Classical languages at the secondary level. The discussion of European identity appears to be more wedded to the historical contribution of Christianity, as evidenced by the problematical incorporation of non-Christian countries into the European Union.

It is our understanding that, in view of this reality, an emphasis on the exclusively Classical register of the European matrix would be reductive, and that, therefore, more than simply making Classical languages obligatory, the possibility of learning in an atmosphere of openness to all the cultural heritages, particularly all European literary heritages, should be guaranteed.

At any rate, currently government priorities do not favour the Humanities in general, and especially Classics, which continues to suffer from the reputation that as a subject it is somehow esoteric and elitist. The emphasis instead is put on technical and professional instruction, in courses which supposedly correspond to the priorities of the country. Moreover parents and students with an eye to 'utility' often choose their courses based on the premise that these could lead to a career in teaching. For Humanities, this argument is less valid now that the market for teachers has become saturated, which has led to a drastic diminution in demand for these subjects in secondary education and in the corresponding degree programmes at university level.

Education system, schools and figures

At the end of the Salazar regime the first steps towards the generalised expansion in education were taken, and then hastened exponentially by the democratic revolution of 1974. The creation of laws which promulgated six years of mandatory school attendance in 1967, later extended to nine years, created an explosion in school attendance.

The requirement for nine years of mandatory school attendance, which has now become twelve from 2004/5, is fulfilled in Portugal by each student attending a standardised basic education programme until the age of 15. This programme contains no Classical content, except for a few brief segments on Rome and Greece in the seventh year of History (for 12-year-olds).

Until the 2003/4 school year, the possibility of taking courses in Classical languages was offered at the end of the ninth year (at the age of 14), when matriculating into the tenth year of school, the beginning of secondary education. At that time the student could opt for four subject groups. In the fourth group (Humanities), Classical languages were included, available to all students as optional courses and as required courses for those who intended to follow Classics at university level. Because of contingencies in the system, the number of students went down drastically during the twelfth year.

Since 2004/5 the choice has been even more restricted, as Latin has become only a part of the course of Languages and Literatures – and always as an option, never as a required course. In this course, a student can choose, if he or she wants to, Latin (which is taught three times a week in 90-minute classes) as a two-year subject (during the 10th and 11th or the 11th and 12th years). If the student opts for Latin during the 10th and 11th years he or she will still have the opportunity to choose another year of Latin in the 12th year, which will not be available if the 11th and 12th year two-year course is chosen. Though it is no longer obligatory, it will be possible to have, however exceptional the case may be, three years of Latin. Greek appears as only one of the seven options offered during the 12th year, a predicament which is made even worse by the fact that its availability is conditioned by the given school's educational project.

It should also be pointed out that a reorganisation of the school system has restricted the number of schools that are capable of offering Latin and Greek; and, even in these schools, no subject can function without at least 15 students, which will reduce the number of classes and students, which have, in any case, already been decreasing over the last few years. In fact, if we analyse the existing statistics, we will see that in 1997/8 there were 323,999 students enrolled in the public sector of secondary education in continental Portugal. The Humanities were chosen by 74,989 of them, or 23.1% of the total.

In 2003/4, only 18% of students chose the Humanities, a percentile drop of more than five points, while the Natural Science subject group grew by 7 points. The number of candidates for university-level Humanities was published on 12 September 2004 and it shows a drop of 6% in relation to the previous year, which was considered to be a positive result by government departments. In absolute terms, the numbers are even crueller. Indeed, during this period, changes in demographics reduced the total high school student population by 24.8%, with the number of students falling to 243,524, which corresponds to a diminution of 80,475 students. But the Humanities regressed even further, moving from 74,989 to 43,745 students, which corresponds to a diminution of 41.7%.

Within the Humanities, Greek finds itself in a situation of imminent extinction. Indeed, in 2001/2 (the most recent numbers available) only 282 students studied Greek at the secondary level, which corresponds to a mere 0.5% of the total number of students studying the Humanities subject group. Latin registered a loss of 57.7% of its students between 1994/5 and 2001/2, falling from 17,453 to 7,372 students; the 2003 data for the number of students studying Latin are still not available, but expectations are not high, with yet more reductions predicted.

Reasons for the choice of Classics in schools

In an inquiry which we conducted among students of Latin at the secondary level, as well as among professors during their period of in-school teacher training (i.e. as teacher trainees), we tried to uncover the reasons for choosing Latin. Following the actual words used by the interviewees, they are as follows: because the course is obligatory (in some small schools in the provinces); because of a fascination for Classical culture; to discover origins, including those of their mother tongue; because it is seen as useful for other studies, such as Law; because it is a cultural language, important in the context of the history of culture; because of its relation to daily Portuguese life, where we frequently encounter Latin designations (giving such examples as *Optimus*, *Vobis*, *Domus Iustitiae*); for its relations to the rituals and chants of the Church; because it is an integral part of European identity, where we have Neo-Latin languages and many important cities with Greek and Roman names; because it is thought to be a challenge to study something considered to be difficult; and because, paradoxically, it is a scholastic adventure not recommended by parents and colleagues.

These responses, in which arguments about the educational value of Classical languages were voiced by only one of the teachers interviewed, reflect a good part of the current and traditional debate about instruction in the Classical languages, even when young people say that they have chosen Latin as though it were some kind of radical sport. This has caused us to think about the debate in favour of Classical languages, and particularly about the argument of utility.

Indeed, knowledge of Classical languages as an aid to the learning of one's mother tongue as well as other Neo-Latin languages is mentioned by almost all the interviewees. Yet a complete validation of this argument would require the learning of Classical languages concomitantly with the learning of these other languages, which is not the case in the Portuguese school system, since learning French – which in any case is suffering a vertiginous fall in favour of English – can begin when the student is 10 years old, while the Classical languages are available in the curriculum only after the student has reached the age of 15.

Keeping in mind that, until the age of 15, teaching is standardised, this possibility is, for social and legal reasons, rendered utopian. On the one hand, the current curricular design, with its general tendency towards a reduction in the class load and growth in the early study of two foreign languages (it should be recalled that Portuguese is not considered in the EU to be an international language in spite of its being the official language of around 230 million speakers in eight countries), leaves no space for the inclusion of Latin (the only language theoretically defendable at this level). On the other hand, even in the more or less remote past, when Latin was required by all those students who intended to go on to university to study Law or language courses which included a Neo-Latin language, the study of Latin was begun at the age of 15. The fight to maintain and eventually increase the study of Classical languages continues, and it remains a contentious area.

Various interested institutions, and in particular schools involved in teacher training, have recently supported the development of programmes to stimulate an interest in Classics through cultural activities such as school theatre, organised excursions to archaeological monuments, lectures aimed at increasing awareness of Classics and the use of new technologies. The long-term success of these initiatives, however, seems doubtful in the context of a general lack of government will and political vision in the areas of curricular design and the organisation of school systems. And, if some teachers have fought hard to attract students, it must be admitted that many others, deprived of Latin and Greek classes, or having themselves little in the way of Classical training, end up by losing interest.

Programmes, subject matter and contents

Secondary education in Portugal is conditioned by the existence of two constraining factors: a national examination at the end of the twelfth grade and a national programme on which the examination is based. As a consequence, textbooks are written with specific linguistic and cultural objectives in mind. These programmes are comprised of cultural themes, especially those derived from daily life and social and political organisation, and leave little margin for a teacher's individual initiatives which would depart from authors imposed by national programmes, especially in Classics.

In the teaching of Greek, whether or not from lack of knowledge, teachers do not establish a parallel with Modern Greek, thus excluding possible references to differences in the way the languages are read. More could be done here to encourage the appreciation of the way Ancient Greek has been transformed into Modern Greek and to encourage the learning of the modern form. In the case of Latin, the teacher will always draw attention in lessons to the relation between the mother tongue (Portuguese) and other modern languages. However, the restored pronunciation is always used to show how Latin is an independent language from which the other languages have developed.

In Portugal, the importance of the cultural content has been emphasised, and this has as a consequence been over-taught, especially by younger teachers, to the detriment of linguistic knowledge and communication skills. At the furthest extreme, many classes are closer to history classes than they are, properly speaking, to language classes, in spite of the fact that, in the final phase of evaluation, cultural material counts for only 10% of the total grade.

Recently, at a seminar where all Portuguese universities were represented, along with officials from secondary education, it was decided to recommend that a new class in Classics should be opened that would function as an option at the lower levels. This should take place in an extracurricular fashion, in the form of a club or a workshop (for students younger than 15 years). This is seen as a way to raise the level of awareness of Classics among students.

Methodology, materials and evaluation

The final national examination for 17-year-old students takes two full hours and consists of translation, mainly of Cicero, Horace and Virgil for Latin, and Lucian, Plato and Xenophon for Greek. The translation compo-

101

nent counts for up to 60% of the final grade. Morphology and syntax count for a maximum of 30% of the final grade, included in which are translation from Portuguese into Latin or Greek (10%) and from Latin or Greek into Portuguese (10%). Lastly, questions based on culture and history make up the final 10% of the final grade. As a rule, owing to the choice of original texts, many notes are necessary in order to make the translations easier.

As a consequence of the existence of national programmes for secondary teaching and increasing diminution in the number of students, there are only three or four Latin textbooks available, all published in limited quantities, re-editions, or reformulations. For Greek, an even older textbook continues to be employed. Even when new titles appear on the market, especially when there is a change in national programmes, as happened in 2004, in general the same authors are used over and over again, and some of them are connected with the construction of the national programmes, which obviously leads to inertia. The use of foreign textbooks is avoided for reasons such as the linguistic competence of teachers and students.

The more common practice is to use original texts, in adapted or simplified versions, for language instruction as well as for teaching civilisation. To this end, texts in translation and modern source books are also employed. In general, the textbook includes the essential grammar, vocabulary lists (the majority of teachers feel that students should begin to use the dictionary only during the second year), recordings, notes explaining the text's principal difficulties, questions serving to orientate and control readings and references to bibliography, including international websites. In the textbooks published in 2004 the great care taken with the graphic presentation is noteworthy, achieving a degree of luxury and innovation in terms of presentation and a reduction in the number of pages, mostly due to the abridgement of the Latin texts. The choice of which textbook to use is made by the schools in meetings between teachers of the relevant subject area.

After observing several classes, we can conclude that the most frequent sequence is as follows: the course begins with classes to motivate students towards the subject. This is done by demonstrating utility via the relationship that Latin and Greek vocabulary have with Portuguese and other modern languages. The next phase includes a comparative analysis of Classical syntax with modern Portuguese syntax in order to introduce the notions of the declension of nouns and the inflection of verbs. Then the origin of Classical languages is taken up, as well as their alphabets. This is followed by the study of simple phrases and sentences, often designed to facilitate systematic learning of the morphology of Classical languages.

This system, connected to very specific objectives imposed by the national programmes, leads to the problem that not all the declensions or cases and verbal modes have been studied by the end of the first year of Latin or Greek. Consequently, in the following year it is not possible, nor is it a frequent practice, to undertake a rounded understanding of Classical texts. This is because, even with longer texts, teachers almost tend to be obsessed with the idea of gradual advance (taking grammar step by step), with the translation of a phrase or sentence often interrupted by questions of syntax and morphology. While translation is required (often linked to the consolidation of grammatical material), unsystematic oral exercises are employed only occasionally. Likewise, there are cultural and civilisation objectives. Many classes, or parts of classes, are reserved for this area of study, which ends up being taught on the margins of more purely linguistic objectives rather than being fully integrated into the whole lesson.

It is normal for all the schools to organise educational field trips, favourite destinations being the Roman ruins at Conimbriga (Portugal) and Mérida (Spain). There has also been a great increase in the inclusion of Classical repertoire in school theatre programmes and in the reconstitution of Roman *cenae*, particularly in schools where teacher training programmes are in place.

Universities and polytechnics

The generalised mass expansion of higher education has inevitably included the Portuguese universities, the consequence being a diminution of standards, and a simplification of degree programmes (only three years of university needed to become a candidate for secondary school teaching, during a transitional period, after 1971; the elimination of a final thesis for five-year degree programmes in 1974; the reduction of degree programmes to four years in 1978; the acceptance of less-qualified or even unqualified students owing to the existence of a tendentiously gratuitous system of *numerus clausus* in state institutions of learning; competition among the new universities to attract students, or among all institutions once the consequences of an exaggerated number of institutions of tertiary education began to feel the pinch of demographic recession).

In the middle of the 1980s, the three universities that had been functioning since 1911, all of them state-run (Coimbra, Lisbon and Porto), and the Portuguese Catholic University, in existence since 1967, were complemented by new public universities, polytechnics and a large number of private universities. Half of all Portuguese university students ended up being absorbed by these new institutions, which contributed little or nothing to the enlargement of Classical language studies.

The two degrees in Classics which existed in Lisbon and Coimbra were joined by similar courses created at the University of Aveiro in 1983 and the University of Madeira in 1997, at the New University of Lisbon (where a degree in Latin and Portuguese was established in 2000) and at the

Catholic University (where a course was created in Braga in 1979 and in Viseu in 1980). At present, and consistent with the overall drop in demand for all language degree programmes, a drastic decrease in enrolment levels in Classics has already led to the closure of courses in Madeira, in Aveiro and in the Catholic University at Viseu. In addition to these courses in Classics, many of the public universities and some of the polytechnic institutes offer Latin and Classical Culture to students enrolled in degree programmes in Modern Languages and Literatures. These are either required courses or optional ones.

In 2003/4, 505 students attended courses in Classical Languages and Literature at Portuguese state universities and at the Catholic University, a number which corresponds to a reduction of 46.6% when compared to the 946 students enrolled in the same courses in 1996/7, a year which serves as reference owing to the fact that we carried out a study then similar to the one that we are presenting here.

In addition to these students of Latin and Greek, an additional 3,294 students studied Latin in state universities and at the Portuguese Catholic University, the great majority of them as part of their degree programmes in Modern Languages and Literature. If we compare this number with that of 1996/7, in which there were 6,510 students studying Latin in degree programmes other than Classics, we find a drop of 49.4%.

With respect to Greek, we see that 579 students studied this language at Portuguese state universities and at the Catholic University in 2003/4, a number which corresponds to the total number of students of Classics and some enrolled in the Theology Department at the Catholic University, and still others in certain degree programmes at the New University that offer Greek as an option. In this case as well, if we compare the number of students in 2003/4 with that of 1996/7, when there were 976 students, we see a drop of 40.7%.

In the private universities the teaching of Classical languages is very limited. In 2003/4 only two institutions – the Autonomous University of Lisbon and the Fernando Pessoa University – had students who attended classes in Latin, and, in insignificant numbers (a few dozen), in various degree programmes, including History, Modern Languages and Literature and Comparative Literature. As far as Greek is concerned, it is simply not offered in any private university. Additionally, in the polytechnics, and more specifically, in the colleges of education or teacher training colleges, the presence of Latin in the 2003/4 school year was extremely limited: only two Colleges of Education (Viseu and Guarda) offered it as an option in the Portuguese/English, the Portuguese/French and the Musicology and Management degree programmes. All these indicators seem to predict that these distressing numbers, which reflect an accelerating decrease in the number of students studying Latin and Greek at the tertiary level in Portugal, will drop even further in the years ahead.

Teachers and teacher training

Teachers of Classical languages at the secondary level in Portugal had, until a few years ago, a very typical profile. A good part of them were ex-students of Catholic seminaries, where they began to study Latin at the age of ten; others were mostly women who felt the call of Classical Philology, a degree available from either of the two public universities, Coimbra and Lisbon. It was considered to be a very demanding degree and elitist besides, consisting of a five-year academic programme with the requirement of a final thesis, followed by two years of teacher training in a secondary school under the guidance of supervisors or methodologists from the school itself. At the beginning of the 1970s the academic part of the course was reduced temporarily to three years (bachelor's degree) and the period of teacher training to one year.

In 1986 the beginnings of the process of bringing the training of professors within the university ambit were introduced at the faculties of the Humanities with the creation of the *Ramo de Formação Educacional* (the Educational Training Branch), which had already been adopted by the faculties of Sciences and by the New Universities, like Aveiro, where an integrated degree programme of five years had been instituted. Coimbra included three pedagogic subjects and classes in didactics specific to degree areas in an academic degree programme of four years, which was followed by a pedagogic training period of one year, with its practical pedagogic component realised in the secondary schools and a seminar at the faculty; Lisbon separated the academic training from the professional training, assigning four years to the former and two to the latter.

But, in addition to those with Classics degrees, which furnished high school teachers for the *8° grupo A* (that is, for the teaching of Portuguese language and the Classical languages), professionals trained in degrees created by university reform could compete for these same jobs. These degrees would include Portuguese/English, Portuguese/German, Portuguese/Spanish, Portuguese/Italian or the degree in Portuguese Studies, and the teachers who came out of them had little or no knowledge of Latin and less still of Greek; those who possessed a training complement for degree holders in Theology (priests and ex-priests) were also candidates.

This unsatisfactory situation arose from the fact that the subject areas in secondary education are bi-disciplinary (which could lead to the case in which a teacher without adequate training could end up teaching Latin or Greek, even while being kept from teaching the language which he or she had been trained to teach). It has always been contested by the universities, but not by the teachers' unions. It is not then surprising that, because of inertia, the government finally proved itself incapable of or uninterested in the rigorous definition of teaching qualifications and teaching staff in secondary education.

105

During the years of major growth in the student population, and with the sanction of the teachers' unions, there was a training complement for already experienced teaching personnel who found themselves in uncertain employment situations. This was called in-service training and it was supported by the Open University (distance learning) and some universities and polytechnics.

Conclusion

The situation described above reveals the danger in which the study and the teaching of the Classical languages in Portugal find themselves. This is a situation where, in spite of a healthy elite of professors and researchers, alarming signs can be seen: in tertiary education, the curricula increasingly tend to cut out instruction in literature in the degrees in Classics, and to reduce Latin to one of the variants in the Modern Language and Literature degree.

Consequently, with increasing awareness that the Classical languages are in clear regression in the secondary schools, even the Universities of Coimbra and Lisbon have opened classes of elementary or beginners' Greek, including for students of Classics, while dropping the demand for previous knowledge of Latin or Greek as a specific entrance qualification.

In a truly vicious circle, because of this the demand for Classical languages will find yet another reason for shrinking even further in the secondary schools, much to the delight of the majority of school directors, who are opposed to the idea of creating classes with a reduced number of students, and of some teachers of competing subjects.

As such, even if the demand for Classical languages increases in the next eight to ten years, very few teachers will be willing to take up teaching them once again after they have stopped teaching them for a period of years and dedicated themselves exclusively to teaching Portuguese. Greater awareness of the problems facing the profession, in comparison with other European countries, may act as an incentive for active teachers to take steps to do something about it.

Romania

Gabriela Cretia (with Cristian Emilian Ghita)

It is a well-known fact that Romania is a country where people speak a Neo-Latin language. As a consequence, the study of Latin in schools and universities has a long-established tradition. In Transylvania, for example, there even flourished in the eighteenth century an important cultural movement with purist tendencies, which tried to privilege those lexical and grammatical elements of Romanian that were of Latin origin, restricting, as much as possible, those of Slavonic origin. In the period between the two world wars, the curriculum included up to eight lessons of Latin weekly, for four years. Greek was not studied as much, having only three lessons weekly during the two final school years. Things changed dramatically when the communist regime was established in 1948. In conformity with the dispositions of the KGB (only recently made public), which demanded the exclusion from the curricula of Philosophy, Logic, Latin and Greek, the Classical languages entered a dark period: Greek completely disappeared and Latin was taught only in the first year of high school, that is to 14-year-olds for one hour every week.

If we have recalled here the decades of the totalitarian regime, it is because they explain the current situation. Indeed, at this moment, neither public opinion (parents who have never studied Classics and, therefore, cannot understand what purpose it could serve) nor the authorities (the Parliament, the Ministry of Education and Research), populated by functionaries from the same generation, have a favourable attitude towards Classics. High school and university teachers, along with the Romanian Classical Studies Society, must confront today an opposition almost as strong as that of the Communists. We could therefore say that this hostile attitude has a political character, continuing the mentality of the old regime.

To this we must add the idea probably present in many other countries that contemporary society, defined by the triumph of technology and computers, has neither the time nor the inclination to reflect upon the lessons of antiquity. The resulting state of mind of the public makes the mass media turn a deaf ear to our appeals. Therefore, the TV shows and newspaper articles on Classical subjects have gradually disappeared. There is one salutary exception – the archaeological excavations in our country that, however few, still have good media coverage.

What strengths does the Classics community have?

There have been countless reports and recommendations to the Academy and the Ministry of Education and Research, and high school manuals with a high degree of attractiveness. Most important, however, are the high standard of the Latin classes and the attitude and quality of the Latin teachers, who do their job with exemplary dedication, and who are regarded in most high schools as an elite (in a positive way), as are the university faculties with a Classics profile. These faculties (in the Universities of Bucharest, Cluj, Iasi, Constanța and Craiova) have for years been training highly competent teachers, both academically and methodologically able to teach other disciplines, such as Romanian Language and Literature, World Literature, and Ancient History, when the situation demands. Like any minority, we use quality as our weapon in the struggle for recognition.

Classics in high schools

As we have already mentioned, Greek has completely disappeared, save in the theological high schools. Two years ago, Latin was drastically reduced. It still has one hour every week in the last year of the *Gymnasium* (for 14-year-olds). It must be recognised, however, that although this hour appears in the curriculum of every school in Romania, for a total of approximately 300,000 students, owing to the lack of specialised teachers in villages and/or the lack of interest, it is often allocated to another discipline. In high school, only classes with a philological, theological or social sciences profile study Latin, and these are relatively few. Such schools include one hour of Latin per week in the first two years (15- and 16-year-olds) and two hours per week in the last two years (17- and 18-year-olds). In the same classes, 15-year-olds have Ancient History courses for two hours every week. Since high school students study 30 hours every week, the proportion is obvious. It is true, however, that the curriculum allows the opportunity for an optional course of Latin (one hour per week). It is clear how the pedagogical skills and strength of purpose of Latin teachers in Romania are put to the test. In those high schools with a long-established tradition, teachers often manage to form groups of enthusiastic students with whom they study comparatively and in greater detail Latin and Romanian poetry or watch and comment on successful films like *Gladiator* or *Helen of Troy*.

An excellent way of motivating students is organising school contests – local, national or international. The award system, the staging of theatrical representations (e.g. scenes from Plautus) and visiting archaeological sites or specialised museums (in Constanta, Histria, Adamclisi, Iasi, Sarmisegetusa Regia, etc.), all stimulate the curiosity and interest of the young in the ancient world.

The usual means of evaluation are the grades given every semester and, should students opt for this discipline at the high school graduation examination (in Romanian, *bacalaureat*), a written test.

In high school, the usual Latin pronunciation is the traditional one (uidere [vide:re]; quis [kvis]; caelum [Selum]), as in this way the phonetic configuration is similar to Romanian, which is believed to be an important strategy used to attract the attention of students. At university level however, the pronunciation most frequently used is *pronuntiatio restituta*, and for Greek, the Erasmian pronunciation.

School manuals for 14-year-olds include both synthetic texts and mostly adapted texts. Authentic texts which have been somewhat simplified are presented to students aged between 15 and 18. Annotations are added to explain specific grammatical problems or even translate (literally and in a literary fashion) a segment of the text. Other than in these circumstances, however, we generally try to avoid adapted or 'made-up' texts.

Each chapter of the textbook contains information on the author being studied and his time, on the authentic cultural background, and on Roman lifestyle. A particular emphasis is being given to lexical fields and etymology: the trajectory of a particular word is followed, from its Latin roots to its modern Romanian form. An important part of the process is to determine whether the word has been inherited directly or is a 'literary import'. In the last few years, a number of new textbooks have appeared on the market, each trying to offer more information and to appear more attractive. For the future, we hope for improved quality of printing so that pictures and images (mosaics, statues, coins, ruins, landscapes, etc.) may display their full charm.

Certainly, as far as the authors proposed are concerned, neither the great historians (Caesar is considered easy, Sallust and Tacitus difficult, but readable nevertheless), nor Cicero, nor the epic, lyric and satirical poets, nor the authors of novels could be omitted. For the well-known reason of his exile to Tomis in Romania, Ovid must be read. Naturally, authors like Persius or Ammianus Marcellinus could not be and are not studied in high school. In order to illustrate late and Christian Latin, we offer fragments from the New Testament or hymns of St Ambrosius. As the Romanian prince Dimitrie Cantemir (who lived in the eighteenth century) also wrote in Latin (*Descriptio Moldaviae*, for example), fragments of his works are naturally included in manuals.

Classics at university level

A short evaluation of Greek and Latin studies at university level might also be of use. Caesar is generally considered the best author to accompany students into their first year of university study at the age of 19, because his clarity of syntax and purity of vocabulary greatly facilitate their task of adapting to the higher level of understanding of Latin required at this level. Cicero, the writer most extensively studied, would then follow, his rhetorical and philosophical works, speeches and letters being highly praised for their stylistic excellence. Petronius is next, as his work not only provides unique insights into Roman society of the first century CE and proves one of the most vivacious novels of the world literature, but also offers interesting information about Vulgar Latin, the basis of the Romance languages. Seneca, his much more serious contemporary, is also studied, though his tragedies are seldom given much attention. The Romanian Classics School tends to consider Tacitus the greatest Roman prose writer and, consequently, his work is given a place of honour in the curriculum. Apuleius's novel, *Metamorphoseon*, is also given due attention, as are the works of St Augustine. Of the poets, Virgil (mostly *Aeneid*) and Ovid (with predictable emphasis on his *Tristia* and *Pontica*, which he wrote in Tomis, our Constanţa) are the most popular, though Catullus and Horace, too, have their place in the curriculum. Christian hymns may sometimes be used as illustrative texts, but only sporadically. Martial and Juvenal are unfortunately overlooked most of the time. Some teachers, particularly those who do not underestimate the effect of a smile during class, read fragments from Latin versions of some popular children's books (such as Winnie-the-Pooh, Asterix and Obelix, and Harry Potter), in the guise of a reward at the end of the school year.

The first Greek text to be studied in university (and in most cases the first Greek text students set their eyes on) is that of the New Testament, soon followed by Xenophon's *Anabasis* and Lucian's *Dialogues*, all of which are simple enough for beginners. Plato is next (Plato the writer being given pre-eminence over Plato the philosopher), accompanied by Plutarch, whose variety of subjects and style demands lengthy study. Thucydides, being considered rather difficult, is reserved for the last year of university. Of the poets, due attention is given to Homer. The lyric poets are all compressed into one semester, but the tragic poets (especially Sophocles) and Aristophanes enjoy much more favour. The missing colossi, Demosthenes and Apollonius of Rhodes, although unanimously applauded, are considered too difficult at this level.

It must be said that in the university, students are encouraged to conduct their own academic research. The results, sometimes absolutely spectacular (works presented publicly at the Scientific Circle, bachelor degree and master degree theses) have been recently published by the University of Bucharest Press.

How do teachers take account of the modern world?

The answer to this is, naturally, the free access to the internet and watching every theatrical performance based on Classical plays, which are fortunately quite numerous in Romania.

As far as modern languages are concerned, the most important foreign language in Romania is English, which occupies the place once held by

French. German has rapidly increased in importance, as have (although less spectacularly) Spanish and Italian.

We believe that a solid knowledge of Latin and Greek improves the mastery of any modern language. On the one hand, no language spoken today can avoid the influence of the Classical languages on its vocabulary, not only because the great majority of the so-called 'international words' (those that, with only slight modification of spelling, can be used in most countries: e.g. English *ideology*, French *idéologie*, German *Ideologie*, Italian *ideologia*, Portuguese *ideologia*, Romanian *ideologie*, Spanish *ideología*) come from either Latin or Greek, but also because the very patterns of word formation are similar to those of the Classical languages, to such a degree that expressing abstract thinking in any European language without lexemes of Classical origin is all but impossible. On the other hand, studying the grammar of Greek and Latin facilitates the understanding of grammatical categories such as diathesis, aspect or case, which are known to puzzle those not acquainted with the Classics.

This sketch obviously cannot be either complete or permanently true. Due attention must be given, however, to the determination of the body of teachers and of the Romanian Classical Studies Society who do not accept, under any circumstances, the possibility of abandoning the defence of a discipline with such high a degree of utility for mental exercise and for shaping the personality.

Spain

José Luis Navarro

Spain has always been a country heavily influenced by ancient civilisation. The presence and influence of the Romans was strong and so was the establishment of monasteries and universities at the end of the Middle Ages. A renaissance and humanistic spirit meant that Latin was used for many documents, and most of the so-called Golden Century playwrights make it clear in their plays that they were strongly influenced by the ancient Classical writers. Even if most of them were unable to read Greek, they could cope well in Latin and they all had a good knowledge of Classical mythology. The eighteenth century was also a positive one for Classical education, as was the nineteenth. At the beginning of the twentieth century the situation was not as good as it had been before. It was really only after the civil war that Classical Studies entered middle or secondary education. Latin was always present but Greek was not. From 1950 up to the present both Classical languages have been offered in the curriculum. Since Franco's death in 1975, several changes have occurred in the educational system. Each time the government changes, alterations are made in the national curriculum. For this reason I shall speak only about the present situation, even though the socialist government elected in 2004 has promised a new education law, the fourth reform in the 30 years since Franco's death.

Curriculum

- Latin is not compulsory anymore at the ESO (*Educación Secundaria Obligatoria*); nor is Greek. In fact Greek has never been a compulsory subject.
- Latin was compulsory for every student up to the age of 16 from 1979 to 1999.
- Latin is now necessary for those who decide to study to the baccalaureate (*Bachillerato*) level, following the so-called Humanistic branch, for two years (17 to 18). They receive four hours a week and the subject is taken by 10% of the students.
- Greek is in the same situation. Those taking the Humanistic branch of the *Bachillerato* take it for four hours a week for two years. Again, about 10% of the students take it.
- *Cultura Clásica* (Classical Civilisation), a new subject dating from

112

the new education law of 1989, is offered as a compulsory subject in all schools (both private and public) at the ESO. Pupils who are 15/16 years old take it for two hours a week. Whether a class can be formed with sufficient numbers depends on the director/headteacher of the school. In many schools the students must choose between French and *Cultura Clásica*. In other schools a choice must be made from a long list of often diverse subjects.

The Latin and Greek courses consist mostly of language work: grammar and a lot of vocabulary, together with translation of texts. However, these texts should always be seen in the context of Latin and Greek civilisation.

Cultura Clásica, on the other hand, does not deal with grammar at all. In the second year there is some study of vocabulary.

A wide range of texts is offered but the official programme suggests:
- Texts from the republican and imperial periods: first century BCE and first century CE (not including poetry).
- Classical prose writers of the fifth and fourth centuries BCE for Greek, although Pausanias, Plutarch and Apollodorus are admitted.
- Medieval Latin, Modern Greek (Byzantine or *koine*), and even Vulgar Latin are not included at all.

A Classical pronunciation (*pronuntiatio restituta*) is followed for Latin (not ecclesiastical Latin, nor a Spanish pronunciation). The pronunciation of Erasmus is used for Greek.

Methods and textbooks

Most of the contemporary textbooks are very well produced but the majority follow traditional grammatical systems. Although *Reading Greek* (Jones and Sidwell 1978) and *Reading Latin* (Jones and Sidwell 1986) were translated into Spanish several years ago, they have not been very successful. In fact students who for two years followed the programme of *Reading Greek* were unable to translate the official examination text of Thucydides in 1990. At the same time those who followed traditional methods were unable to cope with ten lines of a passage in *Reading Greek*. This incident was reported by teachers at Seville University and perhaps goes to show how far methods, textbooks and examinations are culturally determined.

Most textbooks start off using adapted or invented texts, but they normally move quite quickly into original texts. It is not always universally accepted that the goal of learning Latin and Greek language is to read real texts in their original and authentic state. Many still teach grammar for its own sake, although not in such an obsessive way as before. Scholars at the *Universidad de Salamanca* have elaborated 'frequency indexes' which allow teachers to concentrate on basic vocabulary, basic syntax patterns and basic grammar. These indexes allow teachers to focus on the frequently appearing words and patterns of texts (fourth to fifth centuries BCE for Greek, first BCE and first CE for Latin). Not all teachers work in this way, but grammar is no longer chanted as it was in the 1950s.

Teachers

The situation for teachers is different depending on which type of school they work in. State schools offer teachers an excellent prospect. Greek and Latin are organised in two different departments. Even the examinations to gain a permanent post are different. There must be two teachers (one for Latin and one for Greek) in each school. The most recently established state schools have started working with a single teacher, a Classicist who is responsible for both languages. This teacher has a timetable of 15 hours a week and earns 2,000 euros a month, not including a supplement for seniority. All this makes the situation of Classicists at a state school very positive.

In private schools it is rather different. Until 1995 priests and nuns took care of the teaching of Latin and Greek in many schools. As many of these have retired and few new ones have taken their place, there has been a need for Classics teachers for the last ten years. In these schools there would be one single teacher for both languages who would very often have to teach Spanish Literature or Philosophy as well. This teacher works for 25 hours a week for a salary of about 1,600 euros per month.

Although there is now quite a large amount of teaching material using the new technologies (videos, images and illustrations, games, websites, etc.), many Classics teachers in Spain trust nothing but chalk and the blackboard. In addition these traditional methods give very good results. At a recent examination for entering university, Greek was passed by more than 75% of the students and Latin by 73%. These are the subjects with the highest pass rates, and so Classics teachers boast that they achieve high results even though they use methods that some may find too traditional.

Activities

The main activities involving students are:
- visiting museums and ancient Roman towns
- performances of ancient Greek drama in Roman theatres.

Performances of this kind were attended by about 95,000 students in 2004.

Teachers also take a very active part in instructional tours and seminars organised by SEEC (*Sociedad Española de Estudios Clásicos*) every year. These tours are arranged in such a way that the destination is relevant to Greek Civilisation one year, and to Roman the next. Excavations in progress can be attended by students at secondary school, with grants available from SEEC.

Society and politics

It would be true to claim that each change in the educational system has affected Classics in some way. Teachers have been fighting since 1975 in a very determined way. It is strange to reflect that left-wing parties, which made improvements to education and raised the intellectual level in the 1930s when Spain became a republic (1931-5), were after Franco's death in 1975 responsible for nearly killing off Classics. Latin and Greek were seen as connected to the Church, and the Catholic Church was felt to be almost an appendix of Franco's system. This was true, but in fact the biggest development of Latin and Greek in schools was provided during the 40 years of Franco's dictatorship. The socialists instead removed Latin as a compulsory subject for a year and almost completely forgot about Greek. When the Popular Party gained control in 1996, a big battle started to reintroduce Philosophy, History and Classics, all three of which had been severely damaged by the governments of González (1981-96).

The association of Classics teachers (SEEC) promoted a manifesto, signed by members of academies, intellectuals and some artists. It got quite a lot of publicity in newspapers and television. It supported the study not only of Classics but also of the Humanities generally (History, Philosophy, Language and Literature). Many people today regard Classics as a subject that is not at all useful, a waste of time that could be devoted to more practical subjects. There is a continual battle of Marathon against the Χρυσόφοροι Μήδοι who threaten our small territory. In this fight we always argue on the grounds of the European background, trying to take everybody back to the roots of Ancient Greece and Rome. But it takes time. In Spain schools have been forced to give place to regional languages (Catalan, Vasco) that have been introduced as compulsory subjects in the curriculum since 1981.

University

At universities the situation is fairly similar. At the end of the 1960s only Madrid, Barcelona, Salamanca, Granada, Santiago and Seville offered the opportunity of a degree in Classical Studies. At the beginning of the twenty-first century more than 30 universities offer degrees. Many of them have a small department with a very small budget and a severely reduced number of students. In Madrid, at the Central University, about 25 to 30 students get a degree in Classics each year. This is the highest figure and the average is about eight to ten students. Even so there are colloquia, congresses and seminars throughout the year all over Spain, although there may be more speakers than listeners. Reviews are published in increasing numbers, and publications and research on many different topics grow continuously. A big effort has been made to translate into modern Spanish all major works of Greek and Latin literature.

Course books appear every year, but the number of students does not grow and the level is lower than it was before.

Until 1971, Homer and Virgil were authors for the National Examination when entering university. Those who wanted to take Classics were supposed to have a high enough level to translate these texts with comments on metre, syntax and morphology.

From 1971 until 1993 a text from Xenophon, Thucydides or even Euripides was set for the students to translate and comment on to pass the examination. From 1993 to 2003, Greek was no longer compulsory at the National Examination, and Latin moved from Sallust and Cicero to Caesar. Now Eutropius, Nepos and Apollodorus have taken their places. This means that the level of those entering university and taking Classics is quite low. Sometimes students without previous knowledge of Greek and even Latin can be admitted to a Classics degree. Other faculties, such as the Faculty of Law, can be overcrowded and may require high marks for entrance. Students who are turned down by such faculties may turn to Classical Studies instead, and so they are accommodated on beginners' courses. However, by the end of the second year of study they must be able to attain the same level as other students entering with sufficient language skills.

The future

To take a more optimistic view of the future, there are some encouraging developments. Although *Cultura Clásica* will remain an option for everyone at the age of 15 for two hours a week despite proposals that it should become compulsory, Latin will keep its position and there will also be the same position for the first year of Greek. However, Greek will almost certainly lose its position as a compulsory subject for those who are putting themselves forward as candidates for university. Nevertheless, activities are flourishing and the SEEC continues to be a strong association with 5,000 members. Although this is a drop in the ocean for a population of 50 million, the specialists and lovers of Classical Studies will continue the struggle for survival. As we have always survived until now we shall continue to do so.

Sweden

Eva Schough Tarandi

Teaching Classics in Sweden makes you feel quite marginalised. As a Classics teacher there you teach 'Latin and General Language Studies' as a subject. Very few teach Greek, only about ten in the whole of Sweden. Teachers of Latin and general language studies (*Latin med allmän språkkunskap*) are about 120, including those who also teach Greek.

Teaching Classics implies the transmission of knowledge of language, history, culture and general linguistic awareness. This last would include such things as Latin and Greek prefixes and suffixes, or other Classical words living in modern languages as '*mots savants*' or '*mots populaires*'. The main and most important role you have as a Classics teacher is that you feel like a bearer of culture, both general culture and Classical culture in particular. The aim is also to support the pupils' studies in modern languages to make them compare, and achieve a historical perspective on, the modern languages they are learning, and to develop their awareness of Europe and the world as a whole. At a secondary school level, with pupils aged 17 to 19, teachers normally teach two or three subjects. As a Classics teacher you teach one or, in the best of worlds, two Classical languages and a modern language (English, Spanish, French, German or Italian, for example). Nowadays the subject Latin and General Language Studies is available in three steps, A, B and C courses (see below). At some schools the A and sometimes B courses are made compulsory for students of the linguistic stream of the Social Studies programme. I know of one school where all three steps are compulsory for this stream. At a very few schools you can also take Latin C as an individual choice. Latin A is often optional also for other theoretical programmes, for example the Natural Science programme, and is given as a subject within the individual choice, which means you will teach a mixture of pupils from different programmes and of different ages between 17 and 19. At some schools teachers have tried experiments to be able to give Latin courses at all and then have combined pupils of the A, B and C levels in one group. Sometimes you have to do anything and everything to make Latin survive at your school.

From this you can imagine that being a Classics teacher in Sweden often means fighting for the existence of your subject. You have to work a lot on 'marketing'. Your present and former students are very good ways of spreading the good news and the advantages of taking Classics. Sometimes you have to use parents to start a course group. Classical languages used to have a special position in the school law. It was a government guideline that if five or more students chose to study Classics, the local community (which has the authority for organising education) had to make a group start at one school. In the remote and sparsely populated communities in the north of the country it could be very difficult to form a group, because the pupils would not always be willing to travel 200 kilometres to take Latin. At the moment, when the educational system is being constantly reformed, this special guideline is becoming more difficult to put into practice and consequently it is very hard for one teacher (you are almost always the only Classics teacher at your school, since you have so few groups) to fight to keep Latin as a subject and you need the support of pupils and parents. 'Marketing' is then extremely important. It is important to be always represented at the school's 'Open House' meeting and at every educational fair, and to give information to pupils and their parents before they make their choice for *Gymnasium* (the last three years of school) at the age of 16. As your present and former pupils are the best marketers of your subject, I think it pays to show them and give them a taste of the Classical world. Many Swedish teachers of Classics try to arrange 'extras' for their pupils, such as going to Rome on a study trip for a week, doing city walks reading Latin and Greek inscriptions, visiting museums or cooking Roman food, and so on. Everything is up to each teacher depending on what energy they have and whether they have been lucky enough occasionally to raise some money for a visit to a museum. Most things like this are paid for by the pupils (and/or parents) themselves.

Set out below are the official documents for the educational programme in Latin. The full Swedish version can be found on *Skolverket*'s homepage (www.Skolverket.se).

Aims of the subject

The subject of Latin and General Language Studies aims at developing the ability to understand texts in Latin and providing knowledge of the Greek and Roman cultures and their world views. The subject also aims at giving an understanding of the cultural heritage shared between the countries of Europe, and providing knowledge of the importance of the Latin language as the source of many words and concepts which continue to exist in modern languages. A study of Latin vocabulary, word formation and international loan words aims to build up a base of knowledge which will provide a sound foundation for studies in other languages.

In its teaching of Latin and General Language Studies the school should aim to ensure that pupils:

- acquire an ability to translate and assimilate Latin texts of different kinds, and through the study of texts develop their ability to use established grammatical terms and concepts for describing language,

- expand and deepen their knowledge of international vocabulary and thus become aware of its systematic structure and cultural historical content,
- deepen their knowledge of the development of Latin for Romance languages and its substantial influence on particularly the Swedish and English languages,
- deepen their knowledge of Greek and Roman cultures and their world view, and of the historical role of Latin over the last two millennia,
- develop their understanding of the role of Latin as a creator and mediator of international terminology in different sciences,
- develop the ability to link language and cultural contents to other knowledge areas, and take increasing responsibility for developing their language ability and their knowledge of Latin and the role of Greek and Roman cultures.

Structure and nature of the subject

In the Roman Empire, Latin was the mother tongue of millions of people. Latin has over a long period functioned as an international cultural and scientific language in the majority of European cultures. The cultures which have been influenced by Latin still set their mark on Europe. Latin is the mother tongue of the Romance languages and the source of a large number of loan words which are common to the majority of European languages. The subject of Latin and General Language Studies covers studies of Latin texts, from both Classical times and later periods. Studying texts in Latin is a literary and cultural historical journey through time, which provides knowledge and a deeper understanding of our own period and our own society. The language and cultural contributions of Latin to other European countries are mapped. The focal point of the subject is the study of original texts in Latin. These texts are the key to knowledge of the Greek and Roman cultures and of the ideas which have played an important role in the development of Europe. In order to be able to translate and analyse texts, knowledge of Latin vocabulary, Latin morphemes and syntax is required. For a full understanding of these texts, knowledge of the history of Rome and the Greek and Roman cultures is important. The subject covers a general knowledge of languages, which provides awareness of the importance of Classical language for the structure of international vocabulary. Language analysis and examinations of other foreign languages broaden and deepen general language competencies. A study of texts provides the opportunity to reflect upon mankind's permanent preoccupation with the conditions of life.

Pupils can thus develop a personal standpoint on existential and moral issues. The subject consists of three courses which build on each other. Latin A provides the foundation for a general understanding of the structure of Latin. In addition to a basic vocabulary, the course provides an elementary knowledge of Latin morphemes. Word studies cover morphemes which continue to exist in modern languages. The course also involves a study of some of the central events in the history of Rome, as well as some typical aspects of Roman society. Latin A is an optional course or a course common to the language branch of the Social Science programme. Latin B builds on course A, and in the course short original texts in Latin are mainly studied. A more thorough study of Latin morphemes and syntax, as well as an in-depth study of Roman cultural history, are also included and are a prerequisite for an increased understanding of original texts in Latin. Morphological analysis of international loan words in foreign languages presupposes a good knowledge of morphemes in Classical languages and how these have been transformed by modern languages. Latin B is an optional course or a course common to the language branch of the Social Science programme. Latin C builds on course B and is oriented towards independent work, self-selected texts and simple tasks based on interest and study orientation. This provides opportunities for insights into advanced language and cultural history. Latin C is an optional course or a course common to the language branch of the Social Science programme.

Skolverket 2004-07-02
Latin A 100 points established 2000-07 SKOLFS: 2000:73
Goals that pupils should have attained on completion of the course:
- be able to translate and understand very simple texts in Latin; have a knowledge of a limited number of Latin words with the emphasis on those which continue to exist in modern languages,
- have an elementary knowledge of Latin morphemes,
- have a knowledge of the pronunciation of Latin during different periods,
- be able to translate and understand the content of a limited number of Latin quotations and sentences,
- have some knowledge of the use of Latin in specialist terminology,
- be able to identify common Latin morphemes in international loan words,
- be familiar with important events in the history of the Roman Empire and some characteristic features of societal life in Rome.

Latin B 100 points established 2000-07 SKOLFS: 2000:73
Goals that pupils should have attained on completion of the course:
- be able to translate and understand simple Classical and post-Classical texts in Latin, both in prose and poetry,
- be able to understand the most common Latin words; have an insight into the use of cases and the verbal system in Latin, as well as some syntactic structures,

- be familiar with the main principles of reading Classical verse,
- be familiar with and understand the meaning of a larger number of quotations and sentences,
- have a familiarity with the use of Latin in one or more scientific areas,
- be aware of the importance of Latin as a mother tongue in terms of the Romance languages, as well as a source of a large part of Swedish and English vocabulary,
- be able to identify frequent Classical language morphemes in international loan words, as well as understand their function and their changes in meaning; be familiar with essential features of Greek and Roman cultures and their importance for our time.

Latin C 100 points established 2000-07 SKOLFS: 2000:73
Goals that pupils should have attained on completion of the course:
- be able to translate and understand simple Classical and post-Classical texts in Latin, both prose and poetry,
- by means of further study of texts acquire additional knowledge of the most important parts of Latin vocabulary,
- have a knowledge of the essentials of Latin morphology and syntax,
- have a familiarity with some common Classical verse metres,
- be able to make stylistic and literary comments on some original texts,
- be familiar with some central themes of the Latin authors they have read, and be able to follow these in the literature of recent times; be familiar with a number of common linguistic terms and concepts,
- know the Greek alphabet and be able to identify a number of common Greek morphemes in modern languages,
- be familiar with the main elements of the history of the Roman empire and societal life, and Roman literature, as well as be oriented to the topography of Rome during ancient periods.

So far the government text. One hundred points means, in fact (depending on the budget at each school), between two and three periods of 60 minutes per week. What can be done from these prerequisites? As can be seen it leaves you a free choice of texts and materials and thus room for pupils' influence, but not so much time to reach relatively high goals! After discussing it, many colleagues think a good beginner's text (mostly in Latin B) could be from the *Gesta Romanorum*, a Latin collection of anecdotes and tales, probably compiled about the end of the thirteenth century or the beginning of the fourteenth, *Versio Vulgata*, Alcuin and Pippin, Catullus, Martial and of course sentences and quotations. These texts are all available in Edmar (1996) or in Marcusson (1969). Then you try to proceed with, for example, Caesar, Cicero, Ovid, Horace and Pliny. Tacitus or Virgil are too complicated for our short and, if I may say, shallow courses, and if they are ever read, it will only be in translation. We use in general Classical, medieval and Neo-Latin texts. But we can never do any whole texts except for poems. We do a little of each to give the students a taste of what there is, to open their eyes to what is officially the main aim of the Swedish school: starting the process of lifelong learning!

The pronunciation we use is dependent on what texts we read. The usual pronunciation for beginners' texts and Classical texts is the Classical pronunciation (*pronuntiatio restituta*) of Caesar – 'kaisar'. For medieval or newer texts the respective Swedish, Italian, German, etc. 'sesar', 'tchesar' or 'zäsar' is used, depending what origin or time the text derives from.

There are no national examinations in Classics. To study at university students must have followed A and B courses, which is the case in Uppsala and Lund. Alternatively, as has been done for other languages (German, Italian and others) at some Swedish universities (for example, Stockholm), students begin their studies with a ten-week beginners' course. In this case you can recruit from a far larger set of clients! The number of students in Classics at the four Swedish universities where Classics is available is approximately 300 in total: 200 for Latin and 100 for Greek. These numbers are not the most recent so there are some reservations about them. The statistics for the upper secondary schools show that about 2,000 pupils take Latin at some level. For Greek at the same level it would be about 100.

The most widely used recent textbooks are *Via Nova* (Larsson and Plith 1990), a translated book of Dutch origin, which emphasises rapid reading. We also have *Vivat Lingua Latina* (Edmar 1996), a book based on a tradition in Swedish beginners' Latin books, with a grammatical base for a start; and a recent book *Forum Latinum* (Nordin 2001), which goes back to another tradition with parallel Swedish translation and authentic texts from the very first lesson. Most books for the first year contain synthetic Latin to a large extent. Some teachers also prefer to use English textbooks. The age of the above-mentioned textbooks varies, but they are between 10 and 20 years old, except for the more recent *Forum Latinum*. Most Swedish teachers feel there is a need for revising or updating, or even better writing a completely new textbook, but, as stated initially, Classics is much marginalised and it is hard to raise money for any Classics project in Sweden.

The normal position of Classical Studies is under threat and the subject may disappear from schools. It costs too much money to offer Classical Studies if the groups are too small (smaller than 25-32). In Sweden all education is regarded according to its 'value' and its 'practical' use, that is to say with a very utilitarian and egalitarian attitude. Very few of the Swedish members of the government have a high academic diploma, which seems to result in very little understanding for studies at a higher level. It has to pay for students to have a long university education. Even at secondary school level some think there is no point in taking higher levels in subjects, since the same number of 'points' are given for each examination. A pupil who takes three A courses, such as Latin A, Ballgames A and Geography A, will score the same as a pupil taking Latin A, B and C, in which it is much harder to get higher grades to count for 'points'.

Finally I should like to say something on the idea of a common European heritage. Up here in *Ultima Thule*, far from everything, Classics teachers and students of course see Classics as a European subject and as a help to integrate into the European community; but since the status of Classics has been deteriorating for the last 30 years, I do not think that Sweden as a whole would even reflect upon this matter.

Thanks to my colleagues in the Stockholm region for sharing their experiences and discussing these matters, making it possible for me to write this.

United Kingdom

John Bulwer

Classics teachers in the UK have shown considerable interest in the intellectual basis of their own subject recently. A number of books have appeared which analyse not only the past history of Classics teaching but also the current state of affairs. In *Classics Transformed* Christopher Stray has presented a highly detailed account of the subject from the nineteenth century to 1960 when Oxford and Cambridge abolished compulsory Latin as an entrance requirement (Stray 1998). This had the effect of stimulating teachers to modernise and reform their subject, resulting in the innovations of the formation of JACT (the Joint Association of Classical Teachers, the main teachers' organisation for Classics in the UK, www.jact.org) and the writing of the *Cambridge Latin Course*. These events are recounted in *Modernising the Classics* by Martin Forrest (Forrest 1996). For the current situation James Morwood has edited a volume called *The Teaching of Classics* (Morwood 2003), which contains many contributions from practising teachers detailing the strategies and devices they have adopted to deal with the aftermath of the Oxford and Cambridge decision and the introduction of the national curriculum in 1988. These studies, together with John Sharwood Smith's *On Teaching Classics* (Sharwood Smith 1977), provide an in-depth analysis of the crisis which Classics teachers have faced in the UK over the last few decades.

It would appear that UK teachers have had considerably more problems to deal with in keeping Classics going in their country than in many others. Public indifference and even hostility, lack of governmental support in any real sense, the perceived class divide and competition on the timetable from the number of new subjects available to students at A Level have all contributed to the pressure put on the subject. As a result teachers have responded with a number of initiatives, which have changed radically the way in which Latin and Greek and the study of Classical subjects in general have been delivered. There have been new course books written for the study of the ancient languages; new courses for examination have been invented – Classical Civilisation, JACT Ancient History; summer schools have been arranged for intensive study of the languages for those who have been unable to take them in school; a new course book – *Minimus* – for primary schoolchildren has been produced; and new courses are available at university level for those wishing to start a Classical subject, including Latin and Greek, as undergraduates.

Education in the UK is locally administered by the countries of the Union. Scotland and Northern Ireland have their own systems, and England and Wales are jointly administered. I shall confine myself largely to England and Wales. Numbers of pupils taking Classical subjects are available only through entries to examinations. These examinations are GCSE (General Certificate of Secondary Education), taken by pupils at the age of 16 plus, and GCE A Level (General Certificate of Education Advanced Level), taken at 18 plus. A Level is the final school examination and functions as a university entrance qualification. As university entrance is competitive, with the more prestigious institutions setting high grades for entry, A Level results are extremely important. What may be surprising to many teachers from other European countries is the relative narrowness of the A Level curriculum. General education is thought to have finished at GCSE level and students go on to specialise in a chosen area of study. At this level they normally take only three subjects for their final examinations.

A common combination might be English, French and History for an arts candidate; or Mathematics, Physics and Chemistry for a scientific one. A full Classics student could take Latin, Greek and Ancient History, but today this would be rare. A Classical subject is more likely to be combined with other arts or humanities subjects: English, History, a modern language or a new subject such as Psychology, Sociology, Media Studies, Law, Politics and many others. Classical Civilisation is available as a full A Level among these other new subjects, and is likely to be combined with others of the same style. (It is possible for a student to pass three A Levels and thus qualify for university without taking English, Mathematics or a foreign language at this level.) Recent reforms have broadened the curriculum slightly, introducing a further examination (AS) at the end of the penultimate year of school as well as retaining the final examination at the end of school, now termed A2. In principle, four subjects are taken to AS level, three of which are continued to the final A2. Some gifted students, however, may take five AS level subjects and continue to take four at A2 level. Further reforms are under discussion to broaden the curriculum to a wider 'Baccalaureate-style' diploma, but at present they look unlikely to be passed into law. GCSE is a public examination, externally assessed and moderated, and taken at the end of year 11 (16+ years old). A further alternative is the International Baccalaureate, which is gaining in popularity in the independent sector. Here six subjects are studied, three at a higher level. Latin may be taken as one of the subjects. (See: www.ibo.org).

The figures for examination entries show that Latin has come under severe pressure through the 1990s, but that Classical Civilisation has been steady, particularly at A Level. From the inception of GCSE in 1988, entries for GCSE Latin have declined from 16,236 in 1988 to 10,365 in 2001. Classical Civilisation had 4,227 entries in 1988 and has roughly maintained this level, with 3,904 in 2001. There were some variations in the intervening years with a decline in the early 1990s and a recovery from 1996 to 2001. Entries at A Level for Latin have slowly declined from 1,645 in 1988 to 1,264 in 2001. Very few of these entries come from state schools, the majority being from the independent sector. On the other hand, figures for A Level Classical Civilisation show a growth from 1,708 in 1990 to 3,188 in 2001. As a new subject which can be taken up at sixth form level (the final two years of school education) it has proved a popular and growing subject, which combines well with other similar subjects which are often taken at A Level. There is a tendency in some areas of England to separate the students for the final two years of school into 'sixth form centres' or even to separate institutions (Sixth Form Colleges), where this kind of course fits in well. (For the full set of figures see David Tristram, 'Classics in the Curriculum from the 1960s to the 1990s', in Morwood 2003.)

A distinguishing feature of English education which is not present in other countries to the same degree is the existence of a large independent sector. These schools provide a private (or independent) education, free of the constraints of the national curriculum. They range from the modern descendants of the nineteenth-century boarding schools, with famous names such as Winchester, Eton, Rugby and others, to highly academic day schools, found in the large cities. These schools were once confusingly known as public schools, although now the term 'independent' is preferred. Classics still has an important place in the curriculum of these schools, even though they have changed enormously in the last few decades and are far from being the places known from schoolboy fiction of the past. In maintained or state schools there is far less Classics and all Classical subjects are under pressure. Here all kinds of devices are employed to keep their place on the timetable. The crucial date of 1960, when Oxford and Cambridge abolished their requirement for GCE O Level Latin (the then equivalent of GCSE), was accompanied in the years that followed by a move to comprehensive schools. Previously there had been a mix of grammar schools, which educated the top ability range to university entrance, and modern schools, which educated the others for employment. Classics continued to play a part in the curriculum of the grammar schools, which took, by selective entrance examination, the upper range of ability from all social classes. Once grammar schools disappeared Classics was squeezed out of the timetable of the comprehensive schools by a mixture of pressure from other subjects, a tendency to modernisation and even political opposition. It has not passed unnoticed that a far higher proportion of students from the middle and lower social classes attended the most competitive universities under the grammar school system than happens now. The fact that Classical subjects have managed to hang on in some maintained schools is due often to a particular group of dedicated teachers or even a single individual who has had the commitment to carry on. It is clear from the number of cases where this has happened that it is certainly possible to maintain classes given the enthusiasm of one very special person. In these schools the teaching is far removed from the traditional picture of the Latin master of popular fiction. These are unstuffy, forward-looking, computer-literate and dedicated individuals.

Though there had been central government control of the curriculum in the past, it was not until 1988 that it was reintroduced by the then Conservative government. No place was found for any form of Classics as a foundation subject. The decline in numbers through the 1970s and 1980s, due to the factors already discussed, left Classical subjects in a state where the government could argue that it was no longer in demand and consequently did not justify a place in the national curriculum. The freedom that had been in place previously worked against Classics here. Other countries where the subject had been protected by statute were perhaps in a more fortunate position. Classics has been left to justify itself alongside other minority subjects to be included in the small area of the curriculum which was left to each school to decide. Few maintained or state schools were able to find the time for even one Classical subject; Greek was out of the question and even Latin would probably have to give way to Classical Civilisation. On the other hand the national curriculum did find room for some Classical material to be studied in primary schools. This was to be included in the History syllabus for Key Stage 2 (upper primary), where the 'beliefs and achievements of the Greeks and the influence of their civilisation on the world today' were studied. Aspects of Roman Britain were also included in the programme for the study of British History. In the prescriptions for English there were references to Greek mythology and to investigating the development of English including the influence of other languages on it.

Clearly there was scope here for some limited language study of Greek and Latin (Brenda Gay, 'Classics Teaching and the National Curriculum', in Morwood 2003). Some schools have been able to build on this to introduce some element of language learning. Under the influence of Her Majesty's Inspectors (HMI), the national curriculum included reference to 'promoting the spiritual, moral, social and cultural awareness' of pupils in schools. Some Classics teachers have used this to justify the inclusion of some kind of Classics on the timetable. The introduction of the national curriculum was accompanied a little later by the introduction of school league tables in which each school's examination results were published and a rank order of schools established. Some schools consider, in this time of competition, that the retention of a Classical subject on the timetable will increase the school's status with parents in comparison with others. This kind of action could be called elitist by some, snobbery by others. Others may feel justified and think that Classics needs all the help it can get, no matter what quarter it comes from.

The abolition of compulsory Latin for Oxford and Cambridge (known familiarly together as Oxbridge) in 1960 had further consequences. These two universities have always been regarded as the most prestigious institutions of higher education in the UK and entrance has always been highly competitive. Schools are often measured for their success by the number of Oxbridge acceptances they gain each year. Thus it was important for a school with ambitions to ensure that a large number of its star pupils would be eligible for an attempt to gain a place there. This gave Latin its importance on the curriculum as no pupil without Latin could even try. One stated argument for this abolition was that it would encourage the learning of modern languages. It must be admitted that the UK has failed in this and that its record of training its young people to speak foreign languages is poor in comparison with other countries. Indeed in the mid-1980s Oxbridge quietly dropped its requirement for its candidates to have any foreign language at all, even at GCSE level. In addition the national curriculum now no longer requires all pupils to study a language until GCSE. While it would be false to argue that a decline in Latin learning has led directly to this poor level of language achievement, it might nonetheless be stated that when the British cannot even learn French properly, it is not surprising that they find difficulty in learning Latin or Greek. As can be seen in the other chapters, in some European countries where it is common to speak more than one language the argument for learning Latin as an aid to learning modern languages is taken more seriously. In addition in the USA there is a still a requirement in some states for a minimum level of a foreign language for entry to some university courses (LaFleur 1998). Latin (and Greek) can be used to fulfil this requirement.

In the face of these obstacles teachers have developed a number of initiatives. The first of these in reaction to the crisis of 1960 was the development of the *Cambridge Latin Course* (CLC). The history of this project is fully narrated in Forrest (1996). More than anything else this course book has changed the public attitude towards learning Latin in the classroom. Parents of today's students are still surprised at the presentation of the content, remarking in amazement at how different it is to what they learnt at school. A generation of people who were put off Latin at school by outdated teaching methods and dull textbooks are still capable of putting their own children off starting it today. However, the children of the generation which learnt from the early editions of the CLC are now becoming teenagers themselves and may not receive such negative messages from their parents. Although regarded with suspicion in several countries for its radical approach to grammar, it has been very influential on the creation of new course books and there have been editions and imitations in several languages and cultures. It has recently been transformed into an interactive DVD for use in the classroom, with the help of a government subsidy. This is designed for use in state schools where pupils would not otherwise have the chance to learn Latin. I have known some teachers who have used the reading passages as supplementary material for their own programmes in their own languages. It remains the staple course for pupils beginning Latin in their mid-teens in the structure of a normal timetable. It has an excellent alternative in the *Oxford Latin Course* by Balme and Morwood (1986), which has its own individual style while retaining many of the presentational virtues of the CLC.

Students who come to Latin later and who need more of a crash course in language learning are better advised to take the more intensive *Reading Latin* (Jones and Sidwell 1986), which relies more on traditional methods and uses authentic texts from the outset. This is modelled on the highly successful *Reading Greek* (Jones and Sidwell 1978). The intellectual battle fought out in the pages of *Didaskalos* (the journal of JACT) at the time of the introduction of the CLC between traditionalists and modernisers has perhaps lessened in intensity over recent years, each side recognising that the opposition has something to be said for it. Where the CLC and other new courses have held the field for larger classes of beginners in the lower and middle secondary school, more traditional methods have been found more useful in the increasing numbers of intensive courses required for later and adult beginners. *Reading Greek* has been the model here, combining a modern approach with traditional grammatical descriptions of the target language using authentic texts.

Perhaps the most innovative recent creation has been the publication of *Minimus*, by Barbara Bell with illustrations by Helen Forte (Bell and Forte 1999). The book has the feel of the illustrated children's reader that primary school pupils, aged 7 to 10, are used to. In a friendly and unthreatening way it introduces some basic elements of Latin language. It is reportedly very popular with schoolchildren who often take an extra course in Latin using *Minimus* outside the normal timetable. Some schools are using it to fulfil requirements for literacy and to stretch gifted pupils. The characters are drawn from the writing tablets found at Vindolanda on Hadrian's Wall. They form a family and their slaves using real names, although the eponymous(e) figure is invented. Each chapter includes a Greek myth told in English which can lead to cross-curricular work in art, drama and writing. There are no figures available to give an idea of how many are using it, but from copies sold the picture is encouraging. There has been interest too from the USA, Canada and Australia and from other European countries. *Minimus Secundus* for 10- to 13-year-olds has been published recently.

A Classics teacher in the UK is normally a specialist. He or she will often be expected to teach other subjects and to have other responsibilities within the school but he or she will usually be happy to cover all aspects of the ancient world. Special interests will of course vary ideally within a department where both ancient languages, ancient history and courses involving art and archaeology, religion and philosophy will all be catered for. This is one reason why courses in Classical Civilisation were able to take off so successfully. A teacher with a full Classics degree would have covered the kind of programme which includes studies of Greek tragedy, comedy, historical writing, philosophy, art, archaeology and poetry. There was no question of Classics teachers in the UK being primarily language specialists who did not feel competent in other areas, which could be considered as the fields of other specialists.

Organised trips outside the classroom are useful aids to the study of Classics in school. There are the extended schools journeys to Italy, often to the Bay of Naples to visit Pompeii, Herculaneum and other sites relevant to the eruption of Vesuvius in 79 CE. For students who have followed the Cambridge Latin Course this is usually a popular choice. Writing tablets from Caecilius Secundus' house are now on display in the Archaeological Museum in Naples, possibly in response to the number of visitors who have a special interest in the fate of Caecilius' family. More easily managed are visits to local museums and sites which have special displays about Roman Britain. Museums have changed a lot recently and many have excellent education facilities, allowing visiting groups to have guided sessions with museum staff and even to handle artefacts. All this makes a museum visit more relevant and memorable to the students. The richness of the remains of Roman Britain makes these visits an excellent accompaniment to classroom lessons. In addition the interest of television documentary makers in history, including ancient history, means that at present there is considerable media exposure of Classical themes. There are also the movies: *Gladiator*, *Troy* and *Alexander* have all made impacts (of one kind or another). Film Studies courses ensure that the study of film is taken seriously and it is important that Classics teachers embrace these modern media versions with enthusiasm and constructive criticism. The emergence of reception studies of Classics (study of the impact of Classical literature and culture on later works of art) has been one of the most significant developments in Classics in the English-speaking world. There are signs that this is already filtering down into schools.

Reforms in the 1980s led to the amalgamation of several university departments of Classics, but now there remain a number of universities which maintain lively departments. Oxford, Cambridge and London are the three mainstays, but Bristol, Durham, Edinburgh, Nottingham, Reading, Swansea, Warwick and others are all active. New courses which cater for beginners in the languages or even completely non-linguistic courses attract students who are new to Classics at undergraduate level. Archaeology, Ancient History and Philosophy are also places where Classics specialists are active and where entries into Classical Studies are found. An unexpected success has been the Classics courses offered by the Open University. This open-access institution for returning learners, or those who have never had a university-level education, now offers a number of courses including Latin and Greek language. In this way those who missed out on taking some form of Classics at school, including the languages, can pick it up at any stage in their life. The OU Classical

Studies department, with its course, among others, on the reception of Classical culture, is particularly innovative.

Though this picture may not appear particularly optimistic, there are signs of purposeful activity among committed students and specialists. When Latin was compulsory for Oxford and Cambridge entrance there were a lot of pupils learning Latin but who were not very keen on what they were doing. Now in England and Wales there are far fewer but more committed individuals learning Latin and Greek because they want to do so. No doubt all Classics teachers would like full classes of highly motivated students, but the reality is often that it is one thing or the other: few highly motivated or lots of rather unwilling ones. The places to find lots of willing students are the summer schools, like the JACT Greek Course held every summer at Bryanston School in Dorset at present. Here Ancient Greek is taught for two intensive weeks by perhaps the best teachers available to students, who have given up part of their summer vacation to be there. In 2005 there were 310 students, 72 of whom came from the maintained (state) sector. There are beginners' classes as well as intermediate and more advanced classes for those about to start university courses in full Classics. Students come away testifying to the stimulating and inspiring atmosphere, having met perhaps for the first time other students who are equally passionate about Greek and Classics as they are themselves. *The Times* has called it a credit to Greek studies in England. In the face of the pressures Classics teachers have faced for the last decade or so, perhaps this is the way to keep the flame alive.

Appendix: An Example of Method
Caesar, *Bellum Gallicum* 1,19

Hans-Joachim Glücklich

One of the aims of teaching Latin in Germany is to enable students to understand, translate and interpret Latin texts on their own. This is a high aim and very demanding. Consequently we teach methods that do not demand immediate translation of a difficult text. Teachers no longer make their own formal translations and then simply ask for a repetition of this translation. Pupils can understand the specific kind of translation either written or given by someone else only if they know about the structure of the Latin periods, about the word order, about semantics and about the meaning of special grammatical peculiarities like active and passive, tenses, moods and pronouns. Anyone without this knowledge will never understand this particular method of translation and will never be able even to repeat a given translation. For him a translation can only give a kind of summary. All translations show mistakes and they rely on their times and on the mind of the translator. This is why translations age fast and sound old-fashioned very soon. Using fixed phrases and old dictionaries and vocabularies, pupils might translate fresh and immediate Latin texts into texts that sound old-fashioned in their own language. This is why a translation needs time and cannot be done without a thorough understanding of the text. Nevertheless even an old-fashioned translation done by the pupils themselves is an outstanding piece of mental work because they have to think in two languages and to compare each of them.

A translation of a Latin text can be achieved successfully only if the structure and meaning of the text are understood. Let's use Caesar, *Bellum Gallicum* (*Conquest of Gaul*) 1,19,1 as an example.

Text (*Bellum Gallicum* 1,19,1)

Chapter 19 of the first book of the *Bellum Gallicum* starts with the following sentence:
Quibus rebus cognitis •, cum ad has suspiciones certissimae res accederent, •
- quod per fines Sequanorum Helvetios traduxisset, •
- quod obsides inter eos dandos curasset, •
- quod ea omnia non modo iniussu suo et civitatis, sed etiam • inscientibus ipsis • fecisset, •

- quod a magistratu Haeduorum accusaretur, •
satis esse causae • arbitrabatur •, quare in eum aut ipse animadverteret •
aut • civitatem animadvertere • iuberet. •

Analysing and dividing

The periods can be divided into several small sections or segments (cola). This matches the way Roman readers read and understood. Their texts were written in small columns and the Romans read while speaking half aloud (*sotto voce*); this made it necessary to breathe and to stop often. It also matches the needs of modern readers who are not accustomed to long periods.

To achieve an arrangement of cola it is necessary to underline the verbs and to circle the conjunctions (here substituted by bold print). Every verb is the nucleus of a clause or a part of a clause and conjunctions, infinitives and participles show that there is not a main clause but a subordinate part of the period.

[Quibus rebus cognitis]•, **cum** ad has suspiciones certissimae res accederent, •
- **quod** per fines Sequanorum Helvetios traduxisset, •
- **quod** [obsides inter eos dandos] curasset, •
- **quod** ea omnia non modo iniussu suo et civitatis, sed etiam • [inscientibus ipsis] • fecisset, •
- **quod** a magistratu Haeduorum accusaretur, •
[satis esse causae] • arbitrabatur •, [**quare** in eum aut ipse animadverteret • aut • civitatem animadvertere • iuberet.] •

Colometrical arrangement

This arrangement can be done together with or followed by a survey of the content. The survey for Caesar, *Bellum Gallicum* 1,19,1 would look like this (S = subordinate, M = main clause):

1	(1) Quibus rebus cognitis •,	S	These facts were found out
2	cum ad has suspiciones certissimae res accederent, •	S	very clear facts were added to those suspicions
3	- quod per fines Sequanorum Helvetios traduxisset, •	S	he had led the Helvetians through the country of the Sequanes
4	- quod	S	
5	obsides inter eos dandos	S	guarantors were exchanged between them
6	curasset, •	S	he had provided for that
7	- quod ea omnia non modo iniussu suo et civitatis, sed etiam •	S	(see 9)
8	inscientibus ipsis •	S	they did not have any knowledge about that

9	fecisset, •	S	he had done all this not only without his order and without the order of his state but also ...
10	- quod a magistratu Haeduorum accusaretur, •	S	he was accused by the authorities of the Haeduans
11	satis esse causae •	S	there was reason enough
12	arbitrabatur •,	M	this was his well-founded opinion
13	quare in eum aut ipse animadverteret • aut •	S	either to proceed against him by himself or
14	civitatem animadvertere •	S	that his people should proceed against him
15	iuberet. •	S	to rule

Of course a survey of this kind cannot be made for every period. It is enough if this method is introduced and used in the classroom often and then used for homework. It might be reduced later by using slashes or other signs between the segments of a period. It will also lead to an articulate recitation of the text.

Graph

Often the period can be represented by a graph using the so-called indent system and then described verbally.

MC = main clause, SC subordinate clause; the figures indicate the degree of subordination:

MC   Quibus rebus cognitis •,
SC1   cum ad has suspiciones certissimae res accederent, •
SC2   - quod per fines Sequanorum Helvetios traduxisset, •
SC2   - quod obsides inter eos dandos curasset, •
SC2   - quod ea omnia non modo iniussu suo et civitatis,
sed etiam • inscientibus ipsis • fecisset, •
SC2   - quod a magistratu Haeduorum accusaretur, •
MC   satis esse causae • arbitrabatur • ,
SC1   quare in eum aut ipse animadverteret • aut • civitatem
animadvertere • iuberet. •

Description of the period and interpretation

Based on the observation of the structure and on reflections about semantics and the content, the period can be described and interpreted as follows.

The period starts with an 'ablative absolute' that is part of the main clause. This ablative absolute describes the condition and the reason for

134

the action that is described in the main clause. Caesar's action is based on recognised and reflected facts.

After the ablative absolute comes not the start of the main clause but a subordinate clause. It is a clause with a *cum causale*. This *cum*-clause describes another condition and reason for the action that will be described in the main clause. Both the ablative absolute and the *cum*-clause describe recognised and proven facts: quibus *rebus* <u>cognitis</u> – <u>certissimae</u> res. Four *quod*-clauses are subordinate to the *cum*-clause. Those *quod*-clauses describe the *certissimae res* more exactly. The anaphora of *quod* stresses the single facts.

The first *quod*-clause emphasises that Dumnorix led the Helvetians through the territory of the Sequanians, i.e. he supported their emigration, which in chapter 2 was described as part of a conspiracy with the aim of domination over Gaul.

The second *quod*-clause shows that Dumnorix by exchanging guarantees helped with diplomacy to get the way free through the territory of the Sequanians. Both *quod*-clauses repeat what has been described before (in 9, 2-4).They do not show why Dumnorix is guilty. Dumnorix is allowed to work in a diplomatic field and he did not lead the Helvetians through the Roman province (*Gallia ulterior, Gallia Narbonensis*).

But the two following *quod*-clauses show how Caesar finds a way to blame Dumnorix. The third *quod*-clause is divided into two parts and stresses that Dumnorix acted arbitrarily (*iniussu*) and secretly (*inscientibus ipsis*). The first part of this *quod*-clause is again divided into two parts describing that the arbitrary act was against Caesar's will and against the will of the people and the government of the Haeduans (*iniussu suo et civitatis*). The fourth *quod*-clause shows in part a consequence of the third: the consequence of *iniussu civitatis* and *inscientibus ipsis* is: *a magistratu Haeduorum accusaretur*; this action is simultaneous (*accusaretur*) with the action that is described in the main clause (Dumnorix's case is in court). After the four *quod*-clauses the main clause continues. It describes a consequence of the facts that at the beginning were described in *quibus rebus cognitis* and in the *cum*-clause: Caesar reached an appropriate judgement (*arbitrabatur*).

The subject of this judgement is placed as an indirect statement (*accusativus cum infinitivo*) in front of the predicate *arbitrabatur*: *satis esse causae*. *Causae* refers to the ablative absolute and to the *cum*-clause from the beginning, both having a causal sense. But the real consequence is shown after the predicate *arbitrabatur*. After *arbitrabatur* there is another subordinate clause, introduced with *quare*, as an explanation of the indirect statement *satis esse causae*. This subordinate question clause is divided into two parts, the second one repeating the verb *animadvertere* and so stressing the measures against Dumnorix: *quare in eum aut ipse animadverteret • aut • civitatem animadvertere • iuberet*. Caesar shows his readers that there were two possible ways to proceed against Dumnorix:

either he will punish Dumnorix by himself or he will make the Haeduans punish him. The first option would be easy but would violate the Haeduan autonomy. The second option would be diplomatic, but would be much more complicated. The expression *iuberet* shows that Caesar has absolute power. Caesar is waiting for a trial against Dumnorix, hopes that the Haeduans will punish him, but is considering his own measures or a direct intervention if the trial should not result in a punishment or restriction of Dumnorix whose influence is still valid. Caesar's assessment of the situation is not yet finished as the past tense *arbitrabatur* indicates.

The whole period describes the results of Caesar's inquiries, narrated in chapters 17-18, and his new research as described in the *cum*-clause and lets them result in a cautious conclusion. Caesar shows his readers a process of decision. His decision is based on inquiries, considerations and insights. This is characteristic for Caesar's self-description in the *Bellum Gallicum*. He does not act arbitrarily or emotionally or spontaneously but after reasoning.

Reading Caesar's *Bellum Gallicum* in school

The period 1,19,1 shows how Caesar describes himself, his enemies and adversaries, and his politics, and how he uses his commentaries as means of canvassing for his second consulate. He always describes his actions as the result of rational considerations. He carefully blames the adversaries for causing war and the Roman procedures against them. He uses the Roman ideology of *clientela, pacta* and *bellum iustum*. Whatever he does it is for the profit of the Roman state and his allies, not for his own profit, it is enforcing law, not supporting his wealth and fame. Consequently the themes arising from reading Caesar's *Bellum Gallicum* in schools are: literature as political publicity, promotion of his public image, representation or misrepresentation of his enemies and adversaries, theory of *bellum iustum*. These themes can be treated separately by reading several short segments of about five chapters each or altogether by reading a longer section, e.g. 1, 1-20 and 27.

In addition, the impact of these themes on European thinking and rationalism is considered. Caesar's War in Gaul not only changed and constituted the borders between Celts and Germans, and established a road system of which we have remains even today, but his *Bellum Gallicum* is considered to be the model of European rationalism that can be seen best in his arguments concerning forces of circumstance and justification for war.

This is why we combine the methods shown above of analysing and interpreting a text with so-called productive reception and action-oriented teaching.

Students work on texts arguing against Caesar, on characterisations and polls, write newspapers, scenarios, radio plays and interviews, play reporters and press spokesmen for Caesar and for his enemies, even organise hearings and trials. All these are ways of arguing *pro* and *contra*, of showing Caesar's methods of manipulating his readers and of refusing or accepting or justifying Caesar's thoughts. The personality of Caesar as derived from his texts can be compared with his characterisation in comics (Asterix), plays (Shakespeare, Brecht) and films (*Julius Caesar*, dir. Joseph L. Mankiewicz, 1953; *Julius Caesar*, dir. Stuart Burge, 1970; *Julius Caesar*, dir. Ulrich Edel, 2002; *Caesar and Cleopatra*, dir. Gabriel Pascal, 1946; *Cleopatra*, dir. Cecil B. DeMille, 1934; *Cleopatra*, dir. Joseph L. Mankiewicz, 1963; *Cleopatra*, dir. Franc Roddam, 1999).

Bibliography

Allen, W.S. (1978), *Vox Latina* (2nd edn), Cambridge University Press.

Balme, M. and Morwood, J. (1986), *Oxford Latin Course*, Oxford University Press.

Beard, M. (1995), *What Classics has to Teach*, Supplement No. 4808, 26 May.

Beard, M. (2004), 'Review of *Dionysus since 69*', *Times Literary Supplement*, October.

Beard, M. and Henderson, J. (1995), *Classics: a very short introduction*, Oxford University Press.

Bell, B. and Forte, H. (1999), *Minimus*, Cambridge University Press.

Bell, B. and Forte, H. (2005), *Minimus Secundus*, Cambridge University Press.

Bernal, M. (1987), *Black Athena: the Afroasiatic roots of Classical civilization*, vol. 1, Free Association Books.

Bertram, A., Manfred Blank, B. and Erasmus-Sarholz, G. (1995), *Salvete, Texte und Übungen. Band 1. Lektionen 1–30*, Cornelsen.

Bettini, M. (1995/2001), *I classici nell'età dell'indiscrezione*, 1995 Einaudi / *Classical Indiscretions* (trans. J. MacManamon), 2001 Duckworth.

Brandes, J., Gaul, D. and Steinhilber, J. (1995), *Arcus Teil I*, Diesterweg.

Cambridge Latin Course (first published 1970 and revised in a colour edition 1999-2003), Cambridge University Press.

Centre Jean Gol (2005), *Les enjeux de la querelle du latin*, Les Cahiers du Centre Jean Gol.

CRAC (Careers Research and Advisory Centre) (2003), *Degree Course Guide to Classics, Theology and Religious Studies*, Series 1,3, Trotman.

Crump, L. (forthcoming), 'The much disputed role and relevance of Latin in Dutch gymnasia', in Lister, R. (forthcoming).

Davis, Hanson V. and Heath, J. (1998), *Who Killed Homer?* Free Press.

Decreus, F. (ed.) (2002), *New Classics for a New Century?* Didactica Classica Gandensia 42-200.

Du Bois, P. (2001), *Trojan Horses: saving Classics from the conservatives*, New York University Press.

Edmar, S. (1996), *Vivat Lingua Latina*, Almqvist & Wiksell.

Elliger, W., Fink, G. and Heil, G. (1982), *Kantharos*, Klett.

Fink, G. and Maier, F. (1995), *Cursus continuus*, Lindauer.

Fisser, C., van den Heuvel, A. and Verhoeven, P. (2000), *Roma*, Hermaion, Lunteren.

Forrest, M. (1996), *Modernising the Classics: a study in curriculum development*, University of Exeter Press.

Glücklich, H.-J. (1993), *Lateinunterricht. Didaktik und Methodik*, 2nd rev. edn (1st edn 1978), Vandenhoeck & Ruprecht.

Hall, E., Macintosh, F. and Wrigley, A. (2004), *Dionysus since 69*, Oxford University Press.

Heilmann, W., Roeske K. and Walther, R. (1988), *Lexis*, Diesterweg.

Hissek, O. and Kautzky, W. (2005), *Medias in res!* Veritas.

Hupperts, C., Jans, E., Jeurissen-Boomgaard, S., Backer, M., van Eckeren, X.,

Bibliography

Frank, R., Kautzky, W. and Hissek, O. (2004), *Ludus 1 – Lateinlehrgang für das 1. Lernjahr* öbvhpt Verlagsgesellschaft.

Jans, E., Hupperts, C., Stork, P., Avedissian, K., van Dolen, H., Rijksbaron, A. and Sieswerda, D. (2004), *Pallas, Griekse taal en cultuur*, Eisma.

Jones, P. and Sidwell, K. (1978), *Reading Greek*, Cambridge University Press.

Jones, P. and Sidwell, K. (1986), *Reading Latin*, Cambridge University Press.

Kautzky, W. and Hissek, O. (2004), *Ludus*, öbvhpt Verlagsgesellschaft Wien.

LaFleur, R.A. (1998), *Latin for the 21st Century: from concept to classroom*, Scott Foresman-Addison Wesley.

Larsson, L.A. and Plith, H. (1990), *Via Nova 1* (adapted from the Dutch original) Bonniers.

Leary, T.J. (2004), 'Goodbye to all that, Mr Chips', *Journal of Classics Teaching*, JACT.

Lenssen, S. and van't Wout, R. (2004), *Fortuna, taal en culuur van de Romeinen*, Eisma.

Lister, R. (forthcoming), Proceedings of the Conference, Meeting the Challenge – European Perspectives on Teaching and Learning Latin, held in Cambridge, July 2005.

Livadaras, N. (ed.) (2002), *Homer and European Literature*, Papers of the Euroclassica Conference 1997, Chios.

Maier, F. (1979, 1984, 1985), *Lateinunterricht zwischen Tradition und Fortschritt*, 3 vols, vol. 1: 1979, vol. 2: 1984, vol. 3: 1985, Bamberg.

Maier, F. (ed.) (1999), *Hellas*, Buchner.

Mandruzzato, E. (1989), *Il Piacere del Latino*, Mondadori.

Marcusson, O. (1969), *Med lärde på latin*, D. Norberg.

Martin, P. (2002), 'L'enseignement classique en France à l'aube du troisième millénaire' in Decreus (2002).

Matthiesen, K. (1988), *On the Position of the Classical Languages in the Federal Republic of Germany*, JACT Review Second Series No. 4, Summer.

Miraglia, L. (1996), *Come (non) si insegna il latino*, Micro Mega Dalla parte della giustizia 5/96, p. 217.

Morwood, J. (ed.) (2003), *The Teaching of Classics*, Cambridge University Press.

Müller, A. and Schauer, M. (1994), *Bibliographie für den Lateinunterricht*, Clavis Didactica Latina.

Müller, A. and Schauer, M. (1996), *Bibliographie für den Griechischunterricht*, Clavis Didactica Graeca.

Nascimento, A. (2002), 'A la recherche d'un canon pour aujourd'hui: les classiques de toujours pour des temps nouveaux,' in Decreus (2002).

Nickel, R. (1978), *Die Alten Sprachen in der Schule*, 2nd rev. edn, Hirschgraben.

Nooteboom, C. (1996), *The Following Story*, Harvill Press.

Nordin, A. (2001), *Forum Latinum*, Gleerups.

Oliveira, F. (ed.) (2003), *Penélope e Ulisses*, Associação Portugesa de Estudios Clássicos.

Olschewski, B. (1990), *Classical Education and Society in England in the first half of this Century*, JACT Review Second Series No. 7, Summer.

Orr, R. (1998), *International Conference on the Teaching of Classical Languages in Montella April 1998*, JACT Review Second Series No. 24, Autumn.

Paulsen, F. (1921), *Geschichte des Gelehrten Unterrichts*, 2 Bde, 3rd enlarged edn with supplements by R. Lehmann, vol. 1: 1919, vol. 2: 1921, Berlin/Leipzig.

Pech, J. (1998), *Latina pro gymnázia I*, Leda Praha.

Pros, J. (1998), *Latinitas viva I, II*, Boskovice.

Robinsohn, S.R. (1972), *Bildungsreform als Revision des Curriculum*, Luchterhand Verlag.

Rossi, G. (1996), *Apologia pro Lingua Latina*, Micro Mega Dalla parte della giustizia 5/96, p. 195.

Santini, C. (2002), 'Ostia centum … totidem voces: per la sopravvivenza del classicista nel 2000' in Decreus (2002).

Schlüter, H. (1998), *Lumina*, Vandenhoeck and Ruprecht.

Schüller, E. (2005), *Prima Band 1 Latein-Grundkurs*, Braumueller.

Sharwood Smith, J. (1977), *On Teaching Classics*, Routledge & Kegan Paul.

Siewert, W., Steinmeyer, A. and Tischleder, H. (1995), *Ostia altera*, Klett.

Špaňár, J. and Kettner, E. (1991), *Latina pro gymnázia*, SPN Praha.

Stockmann, F. (2005), *Veni Vidi Didici*, Braumueller.

Stray, C. (1998), *Classics Transformed*, Oxford University Press.

Stray, C. (2003), *The Classical Association: the first century 1903-2003*, Classical Association/Oxford University Press.

Utz, C. (2004), *Prima A*, Buchner (Austrian version by Schüller, E., 2005).

Van Assendelft, M.M., van Gessel, H.L., Molenaar, M.D., Schaafsma, A.A.M. and Smarius, A.J.H.A. (2004), *Via Nova 1 – Urbs Via Nova 2 – Imperium*, Thieme Meulenhoff.

Van der Heuvel, A. and van Duivenboden, L. (1995), *Hellenike*, Hermaion, Lunteren.

Vogel, J. et al. (1996), *Iter Romanum*, Schöningh Verlag.

Waquet, F. (1998/2001), *Le Latin ou l'empire d'un signe*, 1998 Albin Michel / *Latin or the Empire of a Sign* (trans. John Howe) 2001 Verso.

Westphalen, K. (1992), *Basissprache Latein. Argumentationshilfen für Lateinlehrer und Freunde der Antike*, Bamberg.

Westphalen, K., Utz, C. and Nickel, R. (1995), *Felix*, Buchner.

Widhalm-Kupferschmidt, W. (2004), *Ludus brevis 1 – Lateinlehrgang für das 1. Lernjahr AHS-Oberstufe* öbvhpt Verlagsgesellschaft Wien.

Wiseman, T.P. (2002), *Classics in Progress*, British Academy.

Wülfing, P. (1988), *Latin and Greek in Europe*, JACT Review Second Series No. 4, Summer.

Index